Feel Your Heart &

Grow Rich

The Heart-Mind Connection to Wealth and Happiness

by Adriana Rosales

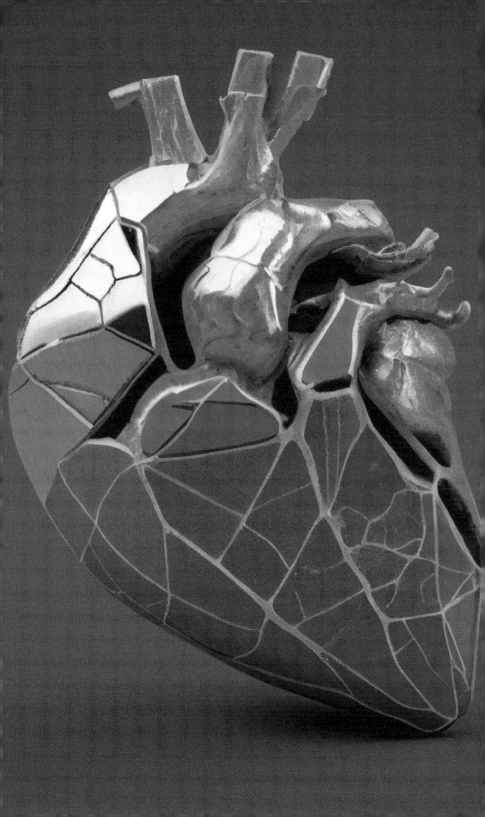

...more praise for **Feel Your Heart and Grow Rich**

Such a rendition from the soul! To know the treasure of someone's journey of understanding life's experiences through the lens of inner awareness and connections to the heart is a most amazing gift, but to witness how that journey has led to greater wisdom and true joy is beyond measure. And that is what Adriana does in this book, she shows us her metamorphosis from human to multidimensional, from loving the light to being the light, and she does it masterfully through real life processes that allowed her to harness the power of the heart. To benefit from the wealth in this book is a matter of course. As long as we are willing to examine our level of consciousness and expand our perception of reality."

Alejandra Orozco, PhD, Co-author of Latina100™ Leaving a Legacy & Inspiring the Next Generation & The Secret Door to Success Bilingual Version (English and Spanish): Florence Scovel Shinn's Wisdom on The Power of Perception and Thoughts to Transform Reality (Conscious Awareness Series)

Seasoned author Adriana Rosales does it again, gifting the world with a beautiful heart-centric book that is much needed in the 21st century and beyond! In Adriana's latest book, "Feel Your Heart & Grow Rich" she offers readers a light yet powerful and insightful read. It is written in a manner that appeals to those of us who are new to tapping into the magic of a heart led life, those of us who value refreshers or those of us who are well on this lifelong journey of a universal love that knows no bounds.

She courageously shares her stories and insights leading us to understanding where we have seen similar signs and benefits firsthand. Readers travel with Adriana on a pathbreaking quest with deep connections at a time when it is not yet "fashionable" to discuss the connection between the heart and the mind. It was an adventure with many commonalities to many of life's experiences. I anxiously await the next book from this heart led writer and I encourage others to read this because it is well worth your time.

Amervis López Cobb, MBA, PMP, SA, Author of "From the Streets to Corporate America: The Power of Mindset & Method: Corner to Cubicle"

"Your heart knows the way.
Run in that direction."
– Rumi

Feel Your Heart &

Grow Rich

The Heart-Mind Connection to Wealth and Happiness

by Adriana Rosales

Rosales Mavericks Publishing Studio™

Las Vegas * San Francisco * New York

2023

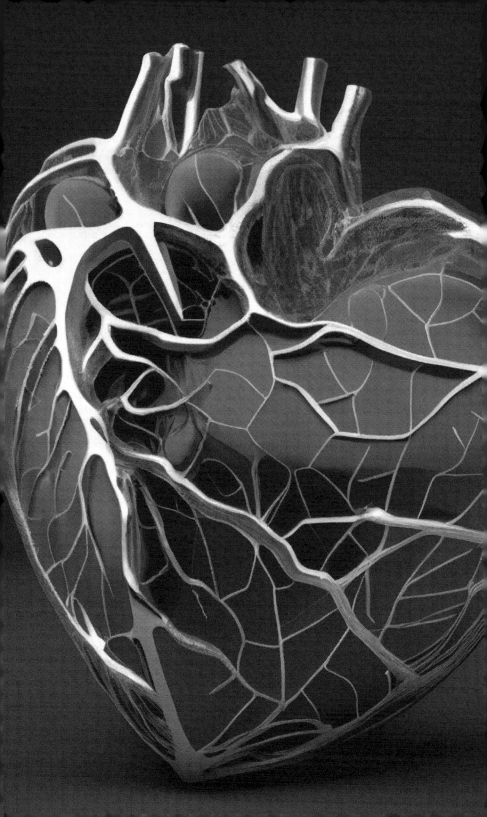

Dedication

My dearest son, Ezra Noah, may the warmth of your heart lead you towards the path of joyfulness and purpose. When you find yourself lost and struggling to navigate through life's challenges, may the words inscribed within this book provide you with clarity and direction towards the things that truly matter. Please know that my love for you is infinite and unwavering.

May you always follow your dreams with a fearless spirit and a steadfast determination. Never let the obstacles and hardships of life discourage you from pursuing your goals. Remember that every failure is a lesson, and every setback is an opportunity for growth. I believe in your boundless potential, and I am confident that you will achieve greatness in all that you do.

My beloved son, always remember that you are a precious gem, unique and invaluable in your own right. You have the power to create positive change in the world and touch the lives of those around you. May your journey through life be filled with joy, love, and purpose. Know that I am here for you always and forever. I love you beyond words can express.

Title: Feel Your Heart and Grow Rich
Subtitle: The Heart-Mind Connection to Wealth and Happiness

IDENTIFIERS
ISBN: 978-1-959471-17-2 (Paperback)
ISBN: 978-1-959471-21-9 (Hardback)
ISBN: 978-1-959471-19-6 (Audio)
ISBN: 978-1-959471-18-9 (e-Book)

Library of Congress Control Number: 2023903669

Categories:
Professional Development | Business | Wealth

Cover design by Adriana Rosales
Editor: Hadassa Muñoz-Rivera
Printed in the Las Vegas, Nevada, United States of America
ORDERING INFORMATION
PUBLISHER
RMPS, Rosales Mavericks Publishing Studio™
1180 N. Town Center Suite #100
Las Vegas, Nevada 89144
https://www.adriana.company/publishingstudio

First Edition
10 9 8 7 6 5 4 3 2 1

CONTENTS

"Here is my secret. It is very simple:
it is only with the heart that one can see rightly.
What is essential is invisible to the eye."
— Antoine de Saint-Exupéry

Foreword

I know the theme and the nature of this work because I can say, both happily and with great pride, that I have been allowed to get to know the author by heart. I say that based upon the fact that I have had numerous meetings, meaningful discussions, and magical conversations with Adriana over the past several months ... magical conversations wherein we shared confidences and closely held secrets, which resulted in the deep and heart engaged friendship that we share today.

I have been allowed to get to know Adriana as the advisor, wise woman, mother, friend, and counselor she has become as an expert practitioner of heartfulness. It is because we have developed this relationship that I found myself drawn into knowing more about myself through the author's life journey to trusting her heart. Being prone to lingering in my head too much, I was delighted to find myself absorbed in the journey of the heart that she expresses so easily. Her journey, which is, of course, unique, still seems to mirror my own and that of many women in today's world where fear sometimes attacks without warning and without explanation!

Heartfulness is, according to what I have read of the subject, a heart-centered approach to life, where you will ideally be able to live each moment by engaging the heart. The concept of heartfulness is to live naturally, in tune with the noble qualities of a heart, enlightened and refined through spiritual practices.

Our author sets up a challenge ... that of moving from mindfulness to heartfulness with the understanding that the heart is "more than just a pump pushing blood around our body." She, as I have done also, worked to examine and make sense of the numerous forces - family, religious tenets, and the growing pains of discovery through puberty and becoming a young woman, entering military service, becoming a wife and mother – that had an impact upon us from childhood through to the farsighted spiritually directed entity that we have evolved into at this point in our lives.

Expressing by way of her heart, the right words flow easily and swiftly into her lexicon. She shares, "Heartfulness is more than just a way of thinking; it is a way of being. It involves aligning our thoughts and actions with the wisdom of our hearts and tapping into the power of the universe to bring about positive change. It means slaying the dragons of fear and doubt with a heartfulness daily practice and embracing the unknown with courage and hope."

Knowing Adriana's amazing capacity for research, study and an understanding of people is a tapestry of behavior, metaphysical and mystical forces, religions and scientific theories, interwoven with ideas, personal perspectives and transformative exercises that the reader can work with in their own life.

Adriana shared with me the story of her roller coaster life including a near-death experience that was a carefully articulated spiritual, real-time assessment and meaningful illustration of the person she is now. The result is a confident, centered, intelligent, charismatic woman, loving mother to her two boys, as well as a friend and colleague to me.

The life journey shared by this author is a powerful account of multiple lessons, myriad reflections, enlightenment, and common sense, with the empowered notion that women cannot only survive but have an opportunity to thrive on so many different levels. Adriana has given credence to the idea of heartfulness as having a more profound essence than mindfulness against a backdrop of mind-masters in the self-development world. I honor her for having the courage to state this concept wisely and bravely.

Adriana writes with an honest appreciation for all of life's mysteries and I want to take this opportunity to thank her for sharing her journey with me. May the ensuing years bring her and her family the peace, love and heartfulness that she both deserves and has earned.

May Heartfulness ... Like Smiles and Authentic Harmony ... Encircle the World

Dr Pauline Crawford, author of "The Power of Authentic Harmony: Magical Conversations Transforming Our World"

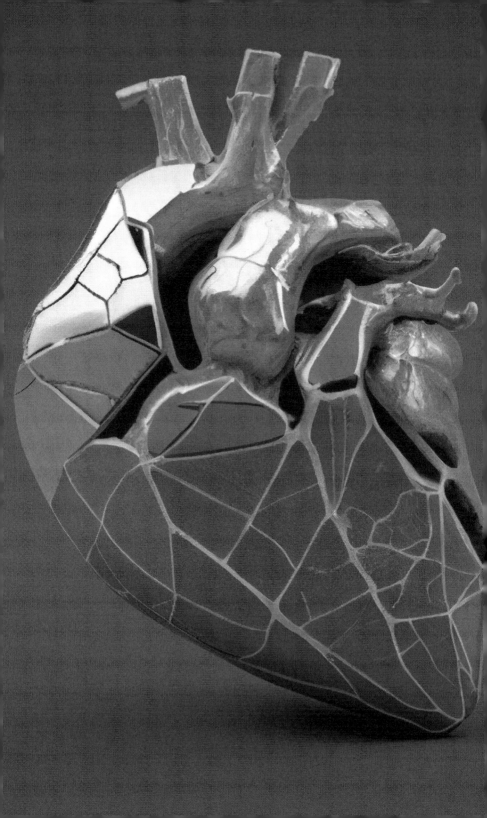

Introduction

Three things cannot long be hidden:
the sun, the moon, and the truth.

~Buddha

As I set forth to pen these pages, I am aware that this is a book I was destined to write many moons ago. Perhaps the sands of time have slipped through my fingers, and my heart wonders if life would have been easier had I heeded the call earlier. Yet, as I pour out the lessons gleaned from voyaging on earth, I am emboldened by the thought that these stories may kindle a flame of hope in someone's heart, and that, in turn, fills me with joy.

The anecdotes chronicled in these pages are gathered from my recent past, moments of transformation that have indelibly marked my soul. They have touched the very essence of my being and have liberated my spirit, and it is my fervent desire that in sharing them, I can offer a ray of light to those who are navigating darkened paths.

However, I must offer a caveat to the wary reader, for this book is not for everyone. It is not for those who are averse to new ideas and new ways of being. It is not for those who seek only to remain in the comforting embrace of the status quo. No, this book is for the courageous, for those who are willing to confront the unfamiliar and embrace the unknown, for in the recesses of our soul, there lies a knowledge that beckons us to transcend our earthly limits and to venture into the boundless possibilities that await us.

I write of a time when death knocked at my door, and I was transported to the other side, what many call an NDE. It was an experience that left an indelible mark on my soul and imparted to me a wisdom that is beyond words. As I emerged from that brush with mortality, I found that my heart had become a beacon, illuminating the path that lay before me. It was a path that led me away from the life I had known, towards a destiny that was waiting to be fulfilled. In the subsequent days, I found myself descending into the abyss of despair, my health failing me, and my spirit broken. But it was in that darkness that I discovered the transformative power of love. Love, the very essence of our being, the core of our existence, the fountain from which all life springs forth. It was through reconnecting with my heart that I found my way back to the light, and it was through heartfulness that I discovered the true nature of our hearts.

I write of the heart, that mystical chamber within us that holds the key to our being. It is the seat of our emotions, the compass that guides us through the quirks of life. It is the portal through which we access the divine, the bridge that spans the chasm between our earthly existence and our spiritual essence. It is through the heart that we can heal our bodies, transform our lives, and manifest our dreams.

As I pen these words, my heart is full, overflowing with gratitude for the journey that has led me to this point. I am grateful for the opportunity to share these moments with you, dear reader. May your life be filled with the warmth of peace, may your days be awash with the grace of the divine, and may you know love as I know it, a love that transcends all understanding, a love that is the essence of our being. May heartfulness be the path you take to the land I know as freedom.

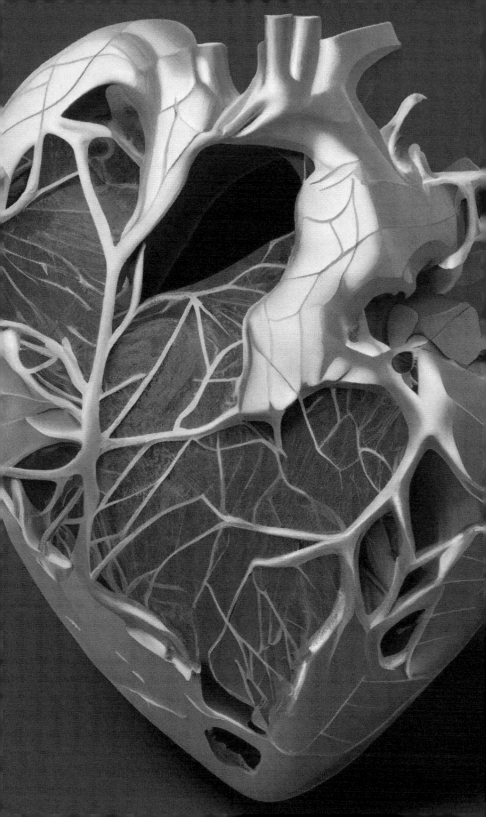

CHAPTER 1

Heartfulness vs Mindfulness: Wisdom Beyond Our Own

Wisdom begins in wonder.
~Socrates

Allow me to introduce myself, I am Adriana Rosales, and I must confess that I once held a skeptical view towards meditation and mindfulness. At one point, I deemed them as mere rubbish, as who could afford to spare time to delve into their innermost thoughts while a ceaseless to-do list loomed over their heads? Besides, mindfulness seemed to be a mind game, a mere exercise in futile mental gymnastics. After all, my mind was the source of my perpetual unrest, why then subject it to more chaos? However, my perspective took a dramatic turn when I was at the lowest point of my life.

Throughout the greater part of my existence, I was overwhelmed by the debilitating shackles of fear - the fear of inadequacy, the fear of divine disappointment, the fear of moral deficiency. This distressing reality first surfaced in my life at the tender age of five, when my parents obediently ushered me to the weekly Catholic mass. It was there that I was taught that every wrongdoing would be immediately subjected to scrutiny by Satan himself. The very idea was utterly terrifying for a young child, but I understand that my parents and the priest had my best interest at heart, and like all well-meaning adults, they did their best with the tools at their disposal.

As I reflect on my childhood, it is the memories of my Catholic upbringing that stand out as the most exquisite. Partaking in my first communion and the vibrant tradition of "Posadas" with my family and church community during the holiday season evoke a sense of nostalgia and wonder that remains with me to this day. These Posadas, akin to the familiar practice of Christmas caroling, were a uniquely Latino expression of devotion. I recall vividly the evenings, ablaze with the flickering light of tiny wax candles, as fifty of us sang Catholic hymns while making our way from home to home. As a wide-eyed seven-year-old, I was cautioned against touching the wax for fear of burns, yet I was guided by the gentle hands of my aunts and uncles, who demonstrated the proper way for a devout Catholic to hold a candle. Truly, those memories are a testament to the profound impact of faith and community on a young and impressionable mind. The indelible impressions left by those experiences continue to inspire and guide me, even as the years have slipped away like the melting wax of a tiny candle.

During my teenage years, I underwent a spiritual transformation and became a devout evangelical Christian, determined to spread the word, and convert those who didn't share my beliefs. I adopted a rigid worldview and was convinced that anyone who didn't attend church regularly was destined for damnation. For more than two decades, I lived in a constant state of fear, indoctrinated with the belief that deviation from the "truth" would lead to eternal suffering. It wasn't until years later, when the pastor of my church was convicted of molesting several young women in our youth group, that I began to question the teachings and my faith. Fortunately, I was spared the torment of abuse, and for this, I am deeply grateful. Such an experience would have, understandably, derailed the faith of most and cast a shroud of distrust over all things spiritual. However, at a tender age, I was able to discern the distinction between spirituality and religion - two distinct facets that often intersect but remain cut from divergent cloth. Indeed, while religion serves as a framework for organized worship and ritualistic practices, spirituality speaks to the depths of one's soul, transcending the limitations of dogma and doctrine.

Through this early revelation, I was able to find solace in the knowledge that my spiritual essence remained untouched by the tragic events that had unfolded around me. In retrospect, it was a pivotal moment of clarity that would continue to inform my journey and foster an unshakable connection to my spiritual self, regardless of any external forces that might seek to undermine it.

In my thirties, despite my high-paying corporate position and the appearance of a successful life, I found myself at a pivotal intersection. I had reached a breaking point, realizing that living in a constant state of fear was unsustainable and detrimental to my long-term well-being. The grip of anxiety and panic attacks only seemed to tighten as I viewed the world through a fear-tinted lens. My fear of disappointing others, whether colleagues or the world at large, consumed me. The need to constantly please others and avoid conflict became an all-consuming mission, blurring the lines between self-care and self-neglect. It was only then that I began to question the reality of my beliefs, questioning if the concept of a loving and compassionate God was true, or merely a partial truth. The burden of fear had become so heavy that I couldn't help but yearn to find the root of it all, to break free from the shackles I had so meticulously crafted and discover the key I knew existed within me.

As I lay in the emergency room at the veterans' hospital, I came to the sobering realization that the way I had been living my life was unsustainable. The lens through which I viewed the world was distorted, and I knew that if I wanted to avoid another trip to the ER, I needed to fundamentally shift my perspective. For those of you who have experienced the anguish of anxiety or severe panic disorder, you know firsthand the crippling toll it can take on one's well-being. The weight of the world seems to be pressing down upon you, and the prospect of death looms like an impending shadow. It is not a condition to be trivialized or relegated to the category of "just a mental illness." In fact, it is one of the most severe conditions affecting 30% of the American population.

When I returned home that day after numerous evaluations at the VA hospital, I began to reflect on my thoughts, and I was startled to discover that 99% of them were rooted in fear. My default starting point was that I had to be good because, inherently, I was bad. I am not sure where this notion originated or how my mind gravitated toward such a self-destructive assessment, but the realization gave me a starting point for my journey. Along the way, I encountered countless mentors and teachers, but it wasn't until I put my thoughts to paper that I realized that some of these ideas were not even my own. They were ideas that others had instilled in me, and ever since that day, my life has been an ongoing quest for truth. A yearning to discover what it means to feel genuinely loved, what it means to extend true kindness, and what it means to be wholly and authentically human.

Following my revelation, I embarked on a journey of self-discovery that was catalyzed by a series of profound questions that I posed to myself. What if the manner in which I think is fundamentally flawed? What if my perceptions of God and my identity are mistaken or incomplete? Or what if my understanding of the world is fundamentally misguided? These inquiries constituted the genesis of a new chapter in my life, and I began exploring everything from the most humdrum of concepts to the most esoteric, arriving at a synthesis that resides somewhere in the middle. Now, as I sit down to pen this book, I am confident that its readers will be permanently transformed by its insights.

But enough about me. Let's talk about Heartfulness vs Mindfulness.

While it is true that my own journey catalyzed my discovery of heartfulness, I believe that this concept merits a broader discussion. Far too often, mindfulness and meditation are misconstrued as hollow activities lacking any practical meaning. However, upon closer inspection, it becomes clear that these practices are about much more than simply sitting still and introspecting. Instead, they are rooted in the profound importance of heartfulness - the notion of being fully present in the moment and cultivating a connection with one's heart. Without this connection, our attempts to tap into our inner selves are inevitably bound to fail. The scarcity of attention given to the critical role of the heart in our lives is lamentable, and I believe that it is essential for the scientific insights into its potential for healing to be conveyed to every student from pre-K through high school. By doing so, we can ensure that future generations are equipped with a comprehensive understanding of the heart's centrality to our human experience.

Heartfulness represents a profound evolution beyond mindfulness. While mindfulness encourages us to focus on the present moment, heartfulness takes it a step further, allowing us to tap into our emotional intelligence, intuition, and deepest sense of self. The human heart, as I will delve into with scientifically backed research, is a remarkable organ that can answer some of our most profound questions. I am not referring to some mystical concept of the heart, but the actual physical heart, which serves as a vital energy source for our lives. Yet so many people remain unaware of the power of the heart to recharge and revitalize our lives on a daily basis. In this book, I will show you how to refuel your heart, so you never have to find yourself stranded with an empty tank. In the upcoming chapters, I will use the terms "human heart" and "collective heart" interchangeably. My aim is to refer to the physical organ that pumps blood through our bodies, as well as the spiritual and emotional understanding of our hearts as a collective entity. By delving into the workings of the human heart, we can unravel the mystery behind the heart-mind connection, and ultimately, unlock the secrets to attaining prosperity and joy.

It's crucial that we comprehend the intricacies of our heart's operations if we hope to reap the benefits of a harmonious heart-mind connection. Without this understanding, we risk missing out on the true potential of our hearts to lead us towards abundance and happiness. By exploring the depths of our human and collective hearts, we can gain insight into the power they possess and learn to harness their energy to manifest our desires. Now, I am not saying that mindfulness is bad. In fact, it is essential to be mindful and focus on the present. But heartfulness can help you connect with your true self and align your heart and mind. One of the most prominent organizations conducting research on heartfulness is HeartMath. HeartMath is an institute dedicated to studying the heart's intelligence and its impact on our physical, emotional, and mental well-being. They have conducted numerous studies and published several papers on the topic, all of which show that the human heart is more than just a pump that circulates blood throughout the body. According to HeartMath, the heart has its own complex nervous system that sends signals to the brain and other organs, affecting everything from our thoughts and emotions to our immune system and hormonal balance.

One of the most interesting findings of HeartMath's research is the concept of heart coherence. Heart coherence is a state where the heart, brain, and other organs are in sync and working together in harmony. When we are in a state of heart coherence, we experience a range of positive emotions like love, gratitude, and joy, which have a profound impact on our overall well-being. HeartMath's research shows that practicing heart coherence techniques like heart-focused breathing, meditation, and gratitude can help us achieve this state more often, leading to better emotional, mental, and physical health.

Another area of research that HeartMath has delved into is the connection between the heart and intuition. According to HeartMath, the heart is a source of intuitive intelligence that can help us make better decisions, tap into our creativity, and connect with others in a deeper way. This is because the heart sends signals to the brain that are much stronger than those sent by the brain to the heart. So, when we learn to listen to our heart's guidance, we can tap into a deeper level of wisdom and understanding.

HeartMath's research has also shed light on the impact of negative emotions like stress and anxiety on our heart's health. When we are in a state of stress, our heart rate variability (HRV) becomes irregular, which can lead to a range of health problems like heart disease, diabetes, and depression. But by practicing heart coherence techniques and focusing on positive emotions, we can improve our HRV and prevent these health problems. (HearMath, 2023)

So, while mindfulness is undoubtedly a useful tool for living a more present and focused life, heartfulness takes it to another level by helping us connect with our true selves and improve our overall well-being. And with the growing body of scientific research supporting the benefits of heart-coherence, it's time we all started paying more attention to the wisdom of our hearts. By refueling our hearts daily with heart coherence practices, we can tap into a deeper level of intuition, creativity, and understanding, leading to a more fulfilling and purposeful life.

As I continued my journey of self-discovery, I came across the science behind the heart and its potential to heal us all. The heart is more than just a muscle that pumps blood throughout our bodies. It has an intelligence and consciousness of its own, and when we connect with it, it can help us to live happier, healthier, and more fulfilling lives. The science behind heart-coherence is based on the idea that the heart emits an electromagnetic field that extends beyond the physical body. This field interacts with the fields of others around us, and it has a powerful effect on our emotions, thoughts, and physical well-being. When we are in a state of heart coherence, our heart rhythms become more coherent and harmonious, and this has a positive effect on our entire body and mind.

In contrast, when we are in a state of stress or negative emotions, our heart rhythms become more erratic and incoherent, which can lead to a wide range of negative health outcomes, including anxiety, depression, heart disease, and more. By practicing heart-coherence, we can learn to regulate our emotional state and achieve a state of heart-coherence, which has a profound effect on our overall well-being. This can be done through a variety of techniques, including deep breathing, visualization, and focusing on positive emotions such as gratitude, love, and compassion.

One of the most powerful ways to cultivate heartfulness is through the practice of appreciation. When we focus on the things that we are grateful for, we shift our attention away from negative thoughts and emotions and into a more positive state of mind. This can have a powerful effect on our heart rhythms, leading to increased coherence and a greater sense of well-being. Another powerful technique for cultivating heartfulness is through the practice of self-compassion. When we are kind and compassionate to ourselves, we create a positive emotional state that can have a profound effect on our heart rhythms and overall well-being. This can be done through simple practices such as self-talk, self-care, and self-reflection.

In addition to the science behind heart-coherence, there is also a growing body of research on the connection between the heart and wealth and success. Studies have shown that people who are more connected to their hearts are more likely to achieve their goals, experience greater abundance, and live more fulfilling lives. This is because the heart is the center of our intuition and our inner wisdom. When we are connected to our hearts, we are able to tap into this wisdom and make better decisions that are aligned with our true purpose and values. This can lead to greater success in all areas of our lives, including our careers, our relationships, and our finances.

So, how can we cultivate heartfulness in our lives? Here are a few simple practices to get started:

1.   Practice appreciation daily. Take a few minutes each day to focus on the things you appreciate. Write them down or simply think about them in your mind. This will help to shift your focus away from negative thoughts and emotions and into a more positive state of mind.

2.   Practice self-compassion. Treat yourself with kindness and compassion and focus on your own well-being. This can be done through simple practices such as self-talk, self-care, and self-reflection.

3.   Practice heart-coherence. This can be done through a variety of techniques, including deep breathing, visualization, and focusing on positive emotions such as gratitude, love, and compassion.

4.   *Listen to your heart.* Pay attention to the messages that your heart is sending you and trust your intuition. This can help you to make better decisions that are aligned with your true purpose and values.

The heart-mind connection is a powerful force that can impact all areas of our lives, including our wealth and happiness. When we live in fear, stress, and anxiety, we create a negative energy that can block our success and prevent us from experiencing true joy and fulfillment. But when we tap into the power of the heart, we open ourselves up to a higher vibration that can attract abundance and prosperity into our lives.

The key to tapping into the power of the heart is to practice heartfulness regularly. This can be done through meditation, journaling, or simply taking a few moments each day to connect with your heart and listen to its guidance. When we practice heartfulness, we become more present and aware of our emotions, and we can learn to respond to life's challenges from a place of love and compassion, rather than fear and anxiety.

Another important aspect of heartfulness is self-compassion. Many of us are quick to judge and criticize ourselves for our perceived shortcomings, but when we practice self-compassion, we can learn to treat ourselves with the same kindness and understanding that we would offer to a dear friend. This can help us break free from the cycle of self-doubt and negativity that can hold us back from achieving our goals and living our best lives. In addition to improving our emotional and mental well-being, heartfulness can also have a positive impact on our financial success. When we operate from a place of love and compassion, we are more likely to make decisions that are in alignment with our values and goals, rather than making choices based on fear or the need for external validation. This can lead to greater financial abundance and success, as we are more likely to attract opportunities that are in alignment with our authentic selves.

By embracing heartfulness, you can tap into a powerful source of love and compassion that will help you navigate life's challenges with greater ease and grace. Whether you seek to improve your emotional well-being, strengthen your relationships, or attract greater financial success, heartfulness can help you achieve your goals and live your best life. My journey of self-discovery and search for truth has led me to recognize the significance of heartfulness and its role in achieving wealth and happiness. Through my own experience of overcoming fear and anxiety, I discovered that connecting with my heart is crucial to unlocking my most intimate self. I strongly believe that both heartfulness and mindfulness are essential practices for living a fulfilling life, but the former takes it to a higher level.

In our society, where productivity and efficiency are often prioritized, it is easy to forget the importance of feeling into our hearts. Therefore, I suggest that heartfulness should be taught in schools to help students understand the science behind the heart and its potential to heal us all at deeper levels not just physical ones. If I would have had this knowledge at a young age, I believe I would have been able to regulate my feelings and emotions a lot better than I did, perhaps making anxiety and panic disorder nonexistent. But then again, I would not be writing this book.

Although it has been a while since I stepped foot in a Catholic or Protestant church, I am grateful for the upbringing I received and the wonderful people who helped raise me. Although their perspectives may not have been fully informed, their intentions were genuine and well-intentioned. When I practice heartfulness, I can feel that they guided me the best way they knew how, and this fills my heart with joy and appreciation. There is no doubt in my mind that the heart will always guide us in the truest forms and that the mind will follow rather than lead. *Heartfulness vs mindfulness is ultimately a no-brainer if we want wisdom beyond our own.*

Chapter 2

The Shift from Mind to Heart: A Constant Tuning

It is foolish to be convinced without evidence, but it is equally foolish to refuse to be convinced by real evidence.
~Upton Sinclair

The shift from the mind to the heart is said to be the longest road we will ever navigate, and I can attest to its truth. When we first come into this world, we are so close to our heart that it is like basking in pure bliss. But life has a funny way of knocking us down, and we find ourselves retreating to our minds to try and make sense of it all. It is like a disciplined military general asking a lower-ranking soldier for advice. This idea, I have learned of asking the heart before the head is a controversial one and one that I have become an expert in.

Sometimes, we need a potent reason to make the shift from mind to heart. Other times, we may not even realize that our entire existence is governed by the thoughts and images in our head. If someone had told me that I was operating solely from my brain and that this was the reason I was struggling to navigate this human experience, I would have thought it was utter nonsense. In the West, we are taught to rely on our minds to think our way out of problems, to think our way into a happy marriage, a decent job, or a fulfilling life. But my life experiences have shown me that the key to success lies in knowing deeply what our hearts need and following that path.

On May 26th, 2021, I died at home in the middle of the night, around 2 am. Later that night the emergency room doctor informed me that I had suffered a hypoglycemic event while sleeping and that people often die in their sleep when they do not regulate their blood sugar. Even though I wasn't diabetic, I was facing challenges with my weight. I never thought that consuming a few cupcakes before bedtime could raise my blood sugar levels to dangerous levels, which would prompt my body to produce insulin aggressively to bring my levels down, leading to a potentially fatal outcome. Yet, it was. I remember jolting out of bed as if an electrical current had surged through my chest. My breathing was frantic, and as I tried to regain consciousness, I found myself suspended between two worlds. What I saw during my death is a story for another time, but I can tell you this: life goes on, and there is no true ending.

Afterward, I walked to the bathroom, still trying to comprehend what had just happened. I whispered to myself, "Holy shit, I just died." I was both terrified and mesmerized by what had just happened and what I could remember from this moment. I was terrified to tell my husband, who I believed would think I was crazy, and ridicule me for waking him up and make a mockery of the incident. Our nine-year marriage had been rocky, to say the least, and we were both clinging to something that no longer existed--the illusion of a happy marriage. It was clear to me that we were on different paths. That night, I realized that if I could not share the most intimate details of my traumatic experience with the person who was supposed to be there for me, our relationship had also died. In many ways, the experience of death made everything in my life noticeably clear and although difficult, it may have been the best thing that ever happen to me next to having my two boys along with deciding to become a fulltime writer and publisher. On a side note, Dr. PMH Atwater is an international authority on near-death experiences (NDEs) who has written several books on the topic. (Atwater, 2023) She has also experienced three NDEs herself. According to her research, couples who have NDEs together or share one partner's NDE may face challenges in their relationship due to changes in personality, values, beliefs, and worldviews.

From that day on, my health deteriorated, and I was sicker than ever before. At some point during my recovery, I had ten doctors. My primary doctor took care of the collection of countless tests and procedures for me and tried to deduce what I was going through in less mindless medical terms. In a nutshell, I had an entire nervous system shutdown. My body's inability to function in a calm and natural way was blocked by some type of neurological issue and I was unable to think linearly. My mind was thinking too fast, and my body was too slow.

I felt as if my mind was in one realm and my body in another and the only thing holding me together were the memories of my children, my past and my love for life. I felt as if I was a big blanket, but all the pieces of this blanket were all over the place and I was desperately trying to weave this blanket together with really thick thread, kind of like a tapestry of memories. My dreams at night became terrifying and I relived the trauma of that night over and over again. So much so that I was scared to fall asleep because I thought I may never wake.

My symptoms continued to worsen after my near-death experience and all ten doctors had no idea why. Having to repeat my symptoms over and over to different doctors was stressing me out. I kept thinking why they can't just look at my chart and read through the litany of symptoms and cure me. Yet, none of the doctors were interconnected, they all operated separately as if every organ in the body was different and not talking to each other. Yet at a very primitive level, although I'm ten years shy of a medical degree, I understood that all the symptoms are connected, and all my organs were responding to the same things. Many times, I wished that all ten doctors could just come together and review my file together and perhaps in a collaborative effort would tell me what it was they believe was killing me. Yet it all seemed like an impossible task and with only twenty-minutes per-visit with each doctor they rushed me in as fast as they rushed me out. In hindsight I should have had someone advocate for me, yet I was under so much duress that it never crossed my mind. I believe it would have been helpful if a friend or people who loved me, went to the doctors' appointments me. If anything, I would have felt less alone.

During my health crisis, I found myself drowning in the countless weekly appointments that only worsened my symptoms. Previously, I had never felt so claustrophobic or irritable towards lights, nor had I ever experienced such panic and anxiety in the mere presence of others. Even after I had successfully fought off COVID-19 twice, I could not bring myself to leave my home unless it was a medical appointment. The thought of putting on a mask would trigger panic attacks and the mere possibility of restricted breathing filled me with constant fear. My throat felt as though it were being constricted and swallowing or drinking became an ordeal due to the tightness that pervaded my throat.

Despite all efforts to convince myself otherwise, my brain refused to comply, worsening my symptoms, ultimately leading my neurologist to a prognosis of multiple sclerosis and I say prognosis because there was still more testing to do. I saw the doctor's eyes because due to his mask, I could not see the rest of his face, and he portrayed a sense of pity and sorrow as he delivered this grim prognosis. I could not help but feel sorry for him, as he had to convey the devastating news to me as he knew my life may now be forever changed. Yet, this experience led me to recognize the limitations of western medicine's knowledge and its inability to fully comprehend the human body's vastness and potential to heal.

The doctor looked more terrified than me, however something inside me told me that I would be ok regardless of the prognosis. It was terrifying and it seemed paralyzing, but my heart felt otherwise.

At the veteran's hospital, doctors struggled to diagnose my condition, resulting in countless procedures like having my blood drawn more times than I can count, MRI scans of my brain, CAT scans, weekly physical therapy, weekly cognitive therapy, along the way I had the removal of my gallbladder, and more. Despite this exhaustive process, I remained undiagnosed and labeled with OCD, PTSD symptoms, generalized anxiety, severe depression, and panic disorder. I sensed that there was more to my condition than what the doctors could see, something that could not be explained through medicine alone. They did care, though, and they were committed to helping me in every way possible. I had countless conversations with various doctors, including my primary doctor, neurologist, gastroenterologist, cardiologist, psychiatrist, and urologist, yet their attention and concern for me, rather than the medications they prescribed, served as true medicine.

In my quest for alternative answers, I reached out to my network of spiritual healers. These relationships I had nurtured throughout my quest for truth in all things spiritual. The first person I called was my Reiki Master Teacher Jodi Friedman. I had not seen her for over a year, and I texted her. I was in too much mental and physical disarray to carry on a normal conversation, and I felt like I would faint at any moment. I felt immensely tired all the time, and getting up from a chair or couch was a mammoth undertaking. Despite feeling this way, I mustered up the strength to text my friend and teacher and told her I felt like I was dying. She asked if we could have a Zoom meeting, and I managed to get to my home office, turn the computer on, and soon she and I were doing a Reiki session. As she began to send me healing energy, I began to shake with so much anxiety that I could do nothing but shake my hands. I felt like my entire body was in a frenzy, and I could not stop shaking. My Reiki teacher continued her healing and waited patiently and lovingly as she guided me through a meditative process. After an hour or so, I finally told her about my near-death experience. She understood and told me that whatever it was I needed to heal would be revealed to me if I connected with my heart. At that moment it was clear, I realized I had stopped listening to my heart and remembered there was a time in my life that I knew this was possible. I was afraid to admit that I had forgotten how to. In many ways, that answer gave me peace, and I knew I had been given a second chance to live for a reason. I also knew all my answers would come from my heart and that my heart would lead me.

The session with my Reiki teacher helped me immensely that day. It was the beginning of shifting my language and my questions in the right direction. My questions should never have been "what is wrong with me" but rather "what is my body trying to tell me." My body was simply leaving me clues. First, I felt like I was dying, then my entire body went into panic mode, and my speech was slurred. On many occasions, I could not remember my native language, Spanish. It seemed a bit unusual that one would forget a language, but there was a reason; I just didn't know why. In this session, I also realized it was not the doctor's or even my reiki teacher's job to find out but rather it was my job to find out what my body was trying to tell me.

My journey to recovery was far from easy, yet it was one worth documenting. Although the doctors did not help me improve, their intentions were sincere, and I found solace in accepting that traditional medicine might not offer me a cure. Instead, I sought clarity, hoping to understand why my body and mind were behaving so strangely, yearning for answers rather than remedies. Unfortunately, my health crisis put a massive financial and emotional strain on my marriage, and in 2021, during my worst hour, I filed for a legal separation, which led to a divorce the following year. Nonetheless, this crisis opened doors to a new and different life, and I continued to visit my doctors while also exploring the holistic route to recovery, guided by my belief that our body possesses the wisdom to heal itself. Though I am no longer religious like I was in my twenties, I consider myself a spiritual person living a human existence, and I believe that everything in life happens for a reason.

I now realize that my near-death experience was my wake-up call, a reminder of my isolation and loss of connection to the world around me. Nevertheless, I kept this experience to myself, and looking back, I see this as a missed opportunity to connect with others to help me heal and recover sooner. I am of the belief that together we can heal each other, and this type of healing has nothing to do with western medicine but with our own internal pharmacy, one of which the heart itself is in control of.

There was one important spiritual practice I had let go of and that had kept me well balanced and healthy for many years. I had stopped my practice of prayer and meditation. In fact, I had not even noticed. I asked myself how this was even possible, but it is true I had not noticed that I no longer prayed or meditated. It was a strange feeling while in the middle of my medical crisis I had asked myself if God was even real. It was a question I had never asked before because since I was a young child it was not a question; I had never pondered, it was evident to me God was real. All I had to do was look around. Look around for the mountains, trees, and sky. There had been no questions ever before up until this moment. That should have been a clue for me that something was wrong, that my spark for life was gone, and that the most central part of my belief system was now nonexistent. It was a dark moment for me that I wish to never experience again. It was as if I doubted God, I was doubting my humanity and somehow my body noticed this assertion.

When I became aware of this and became aware of the fact that my most central spiritual practices were nonexistent, I began to pray again and meditate. I have never conformed to any traditional practices. I do not sit in a room with the light off with my rosary or Buddhist beads and chant in fact those practices are super cool, but I cannot do them although I have tried. What I began to do was to walk. Yes, I began a walking meditation practice. Not because I read it anywhere or thought it cool but because when I asked my heart what to do I hear the word walk. So, I did. I began to walk in 2021 almost daily for one to two hours. At first, I could only walk for five minutes but I knew if I showed up at the park that at least I made the effort and effort was a big win. The reality also was that I was too sick to do anything else, in fact, I felt so much physical pain and emotionally drained that just showing up to the park and opening the car door even if I did not get out was a big win for me. I would tell myself, well at least I showed up and that is half the battle. Every day got a little better and during my walking meditations I would ask my heart, so what now? And all I heard was silence and soon in between the silence I could hear the wind and the birds and then feel the sand and dirt getting into my shoes and then I looked forward to smiling at the other people walking on the same path those early mornings. I realized that I missed seeing people smile and that I craved human connection and realized that a smile can go such a long way and be so healing for a human heart. On many days I would walk and cry, walk and cry and walk and cry. I did not know why or why I even felt so sick and why I was crying, but I knew enough to know my heart would figure it out and I had to trust my heart.

My journey toward recovery was more than just a medical one. It was a spiritual awakening, one that reminded me of the interconnectedness of all things and the need to seek answers beyond traditional medicine. I learned that doctors can only do so much and that, at times, true healing comes not from medication but from conversations and connections with others. Yes, sometimes the sound of the leaves on trees ruffling in the wind, the ducks in the water peddling their little feet to get across a pond with their little ones, or the sound of your own breathing can guide you in more ways than any chant can, although I do recommend chanting as medicine too.

The shift from mind to heart is not easy, but it is necessary for our well-being. In the hero's journey framework, this is the point where the protagonist faces their greatest challenge, the "death" of their old self, and must embrace a new path forward. And so, I embarked on a journey to rediscover my heart, to listen to its desires, and to follow it fearlessly. It was not easy, but it was worth it. And in the end, I found a new life, and a new me. If you have ever doubted the power of your own heart then my hope is that my story will ignite you to reconnect with it and to learn what I had to do to reconnect again and gain my life back by simply asking my heart direct questions, by simply placing my hand over my heart and feeling into what the heart was telling me. It works try it.

To this day, I continue in my journey of healing, diligently attending medical appointments and conveying to my physicians the progress I've made. Each time I recount my tale of recovery, although not yet fully restored, the doctors simply offer an affirmative nod and inquire as to how I've achieved such improvements without medication. Some practitioners inquire into the minutiae of my daily routine, while others prescribe remedies to alleviate whatever residual pain I may still experience. Although our medical system is flawed, I remain beholden to and venerate it, even if I have outpaced it in terms of my own wellness.

Presently, certain symptoms persist, and I still encounter fear and anxiety, albeit not to the extent I once did. When they do arise, I appeal to my heart to manage them, immersing myself in meditative practices and reminding myself that all is well and that I am neither required to conform to anyone's expectations nor to undertake any specific actions in order to understand that I am both love and beloved. I now deeply understand that the shift from my mind to my heart is simply a choice. A moment of brave action to live fully and experience being human regardless of fear of the unknown.

I came to the realization that in order to grow and heal, I must confront my pain head-on rather than avoid it. It became essential for me to express my needs and if they went unfulfilled, to distance myself from unfavorable circumstances by bidding them farewell with a blessing. My heart was beckoning me to prioritize self-love and immerse myself in an abundance of affection while still gracing this earth. I deeply believed that I am worthy of experiencing love to such an extent that life must radiate with life's magic and inspire a newfound appreciation for its worth. The shift from mind-to-heart has been a constant tuning of emotions-feelings and perceptions all well worth it. There is a very narrow road from the mind to the heart because not many travel it but believe me when I tell you the journey is worth every roadblock and every set-back.

Chapter 3

The Most Powerful Thoughts: Guided by Your Heart

Truth is incontrovertible. Malice may attack it, ignorance may
deride it, but in the end, there it is.
~Winston Churchill

As I begin writing this chapter, I find myself contemplating the voyage I have undertaken in the past few years. It has been a rollercoaster ride, full of twists and turns, plot twists, highs and lows, and everything in between. In fact, this book only took me two weeks to write from start to finish because I chose to listen to my heart and not sit on the information it was giving me. The most powerful thoughts are the ones guided by your heart. You see when the heart calls you must go. Do not wait because if you do not do what the heart is guiding you to do it may be too late. I have learned that the most powerful thoughts are simply reminding the mind of what the heart already knows. For me, feeling my heart again was a process well worth it.

First, I had to find out that I was walking around like a zombie pretending that everything was ok and living my life through my mind's eye and thought that because I had all the fancy stuff and material wealth this made me happy. It was only some twisted idea of real happiness not having anything to do with the heart but rather an accumulation of resources disguised as happiness and fulfillment. Through some of the practices I will share in this book, I regained the connection with my heart's GPS; I just needed a reboot and for me that was death. Your reboot does not have to be death it can be this book or perhaps a conversation with a friend or a flash of insight while cooking dinner. In whatever way, your reboot shows up, be on alert, pay attention, and follow your heart's guidance.

It took time, patience, and a lot of self-reflection. But as I started to reconnect with my heart, I realized that it was the key to unlocking my true potential and living a life of purpose and meaning. I had lost my way in the murky waters we sometimes call life. I had lost my sense of self, believing that if I only loved someone enough, they would love me back, or if I cared enough and provided enough then my family and friends would love me. But that never worked out for me because the premise was that I had to actually do something to feel something and that is not how it works.

You do not have to do anything or be anybody to know you are loved and you are LOVE. Your DNA is love and you are infinitely loved across all time, space, and dimensions. That is the truth. This is the premise of our true wealth and being rich is all about this. In fact, "The God

Code" by Gregg Braden is a book that explores the relationship between science and spirituality it suggests that the DNA in our cells holds a code that represents a message from God. Braden argues that the ancient Hebrew alphabet holds the key to unlocking this code, and that by understanding the language and meaning behind the letters, we can uncover a deeper understanding of the universe and our place in it. Braden's research on the DNA signature of God suggests that the sequence of letters in the Hebrew alphabet corresponds to the sequence of nucleotides in our DNA. He argues that this is evidence that our DNA is not random, but rather has been designed with a purpose by a higher intelligence. Braden's theory on this is fascinating and it is worth exploring. (Braden, 2023)

So, what are the most powerful thoughts we can have to help us feel our hearts again? Here are a few that have worked for me. These are not affirmation or self-help incantations but rather a series of thoughts that are available not for you to believe them but for you to simply remind your mind via your heart's intelligence that you are in fact these emotions. You see the heart is like a motor and its fuel is emotions. The way you get your heart's attention is by intention and tapping lightly in the area of the heart and by simply expressing these emotions your heart will remind your mind that it is in fact so.

It is easy to get lost in our own thoughts and allow our fears to control us. We often forget that deep down, our hearts already know what we need to feel whole and fulfilled. It is important to remind our minds of this truth, and we can do that by incorporating powerful thoughts into our daily lives. Always remember that it is never the thoughts first but the emotion that the heart feels then the thoughts come, and then magic happens. The sequence is important because science has proven that the heart sends more signals to the brain than the brain to the heart and therefore, we can presume that the heart is the master controller.

Remind your mind what the heart already knows:

I choose love over fear. By choosing to love over fear, we allow ourselves to act from a place of compassion and empathy. This reminds us to connect with others and approach life with an open heart.

I am deserving of my own forgiveness. Forgiving ourselves is crucial to letting go of past mistakes and moving forward. We must remember that we are human and deserving of self-compassion.

I let go of what no longer serves me. Letting go of what no longer serves us allows us to make space for new experiences and opportunities. It reminds us to prioritize our well-being and only hold onto what brings us joy and fulfillment.

I trust that everything happens for my highest good. Trusting that everything happens for our highest good allows us to let go of our need for control and surrender to the journey of life. It reminds us that every experience has a purpose and a lesson to teach us.

I am enough just as I am. Reminding ourselves that we are enough just as we are essential to self-love and acceptance. It reminds us to embrace our unique qualities and appreciate ourselves for who we are.

I am grateful for the lesson's life has taught me. Being grateful for the lesson's life has taught us allows us to shift our perspective and focus on the positive. It reminds us to appreciate every experience, whether good or bad, as an opportunity for growth.

I embrace change and welcome new opportunities. Embracing change and welcoming new opportunities allows us to step outside our comfort zone and grow. It reminds us to be open to new experiences and to approach life with curiosity and excitement.

I am in control of my thoughts and emotions. Taking control of our thoughts and emotions is crucial to our mental and emotional well-being. It reminds us that we have the power to shape our own reality.

I release the need to control everything around me. Releasing the need to control everything around us allows us to let go of our fears and anxieties. It reminds us to trust the universe and surrender to the flow of life.

I am open to receiving love and abundance. Being open to receiving love and abundance reminds us to approach life with a positive attitude and an open heart. It reminds us that we are deserving of all the good things life has to offer.

I am worthy of all the good things life has to offer. Reminding ourselves that we are worthy of all the good things life has to offer is essential to self-love and acceptance. It reminds us to prioritize our own well-being and to embrace our unique qualities.

I am at peace with myself and my surroundings. Being at peace with ourselves and our surroundings allows us to approach life with a sense of calm and serenity. It reminds us to appreciate the beauty around us and to focus on the present moment.

I honor my body and treat it with love and respect. Honoring our bodies and treating them with love and respect is crucial to our physical and mental well-being. It reminds us to prioritize self-care and to appreciate the vessel that carries us through life.

I choose kindness and compassion in all my interactions. Choosing kindness and compassion in all our interactions reminds us to approach life with empathy and understanding. It reminds us to connect with others and to be a positive force in the world.

I am surrounded by positivity and good energy. Surrounding ourselves with positivity and good energy reminds us to focus on the good in life and to approach challenges with a positive attitude.

I am constantly growing and evolving. Reminding ourselves that we are constantly growing and evolving at our own pace and that life is not a race or a competition but rather an experience that is so unique that it is once in a lifetime.

When we live our life from a place of fear, we limit ourselves and hold ourselves back from experiencing all the wonderful things life has to offer. Fear causes us to play small, avoid risks and challenges, and settle for less than we deserve. It keeps us stuck in a place of scarcity and negativity, preventing us from seeing the beauty and abundance around us. On the other hand, choosing to love over fear opens us up to a world of possibilities.

When we operate from a place of love, we see ourselves and others in a positive light. We take risks, pursue our passions, and live life to the fullest. We recognize that we are deserving of all the good things life has to offer and we go after them with confidence and courage.

Forgiveness is also an important part of feeling our hearts again. When we forgive ourselves, we release the negative emotions and self-judgment that hold us back from fully embracing our true selves. We recognize that we are only human and that we deserve our own forgiveness. This helps us let go of the past and move forward in a more positive and productive way.

Letting go of what no longer serves us is another powerful thought that can help us feel our hearts again. We all have things in our lives that no longer serve us, whether it be relationships, jobs, habits, or beliefs. When we let go of these things, we create space for new opportunities and experiences that align with our true selves.

Trusting that everything happens for our highest good is also an important thought to have. When we trust in the universe and believe that everything happens for a reason, we become more open to new experiences and opportunities. We learn to let go of the need to control everything around us and to embrace change as a natural part of life.

Believing that we are enough just as we are, is crucial to feeling our hearts again. We live in a society that often tells us we are not enough, and that we need to do more or be more to be happy and successful. When we believe that we are enough just as we are, we stop seeking external validation and start living from a place of self-acceptance and self-love.

Appreciation is another powerful thought that can help us feel our hearts again. When we focus on all the things, we have to be grateful for, we shift our perspective and start to see the world in a more positive light. We become more present and mindful in our daily lives, and we appreciate the little things that bring us joy and happiness. In the book "Thank and Grow Rich" by Pam Grout she encourages readers to cultivate an attitude of gratitude in their daily lives in order to manifest more abundance, joy, and fulfillment. The book is inspired by the principles of Napoleon Hill's classic self-help book, "Think and Grow Rich," but with a focus on the power of gratitude. Now, I love this book and think everyone should read it and I also was inspired by Napoleon Hill's classic book however I found that not enough emphasis was placed on the power of the heart and the research behind it, so this is why I wrote this book to complement Grout's wonderful work along with Hill's work.

Embracing change and welcoming new opportunities is also important to feel our hearts again. Change can be scary and uncomfortable, but it is also a necessary part of growth and evolution. When we embrace change and welcome new opportunities, we open ourselves up to new experiences and possibilities that can bring us closer to our true selves.

Ultimately, reminding our minds of what our hearts already know is crucial to living a fulfilling and authentic life. When we choose love over fear, forgive ourselves, let go of what no longer serves us, trust in the universe, believe in our own worth, and cultivate appreciation and openness, we create space for joy, abundance, and fulfillment in our lives. We become more connected to our true selves and to the world around us, and we start living from a place of authenticity, purpose, and love.

The most powerful thoughts to help you feel your heart again are those that are backed by your emotions. When I first learned this and understood that it was my emotions that fueled my heart, I knew that now I had the key to feeling my heart again and also gaining momentum on my manifestation powers. It's fascinating to understand the heart in this way but as you will see in the chapters to come this way of thinking about the heart and body dates back thousands of years.

My hope is that I can help you in understanding these basic heart principles and how our most treasured wisdom keepers have used the heart's power to feel the world in a different way and to manifest their heart's desires. Never doubt that the most powerful thoughts you have that are linked to joy, happiness and abundance are guided by your heart.

Chapter 4

The Mystical Heart:
World Heart Expressions
& Wisdom Keepers

The only thing that interferes with my learning is my education.
~Albert Einstein

Prior to my near-death experience, I viewed the heart as a mundane organ with the sole purpose of pumping blood to sustain my existence, and rightfully so. The American western system in which I was brought up negates all things mystical and unexplained. In fact, if it cannot be proven in the language of science or mathematics it is relegated to the bogus categories. I was indoctrinated to believe the heart is merely a utilitarian component of my anatomy. I believed it in my head and mind but not in my heart. I knew there must be more: more to just our linear understanding of tangible reality. Although I cannot fully explain it, I possess an intuitive understanding that there exists a realm beyond the purview of scientific inquiry, one which is infused with a sense of enigmatic and otherworldly mystique. Most women have this type of understanding whether they are willing to tap into it, is a whole different story.

As I approached my thirties, I was faced with a barrage of post-traumatic stress disorder (PTSD) symptoms induced by my military experiences in my twenties, which were triggered by my workaholism. In my quest of seeking to understand, I conducted extensive research and stumbled upon a myriad of studies that proposed specific breathing techniques capable of subduing my rapid and erratic heart palpitations in a matter of mere minutes. The discovery was captivating, and I promptly began to implement these techniques, gradually becoming an adept HeartMath Coach. As I delved deeper into my work as an entrepreneur, corporate executive and now HeartMath Coach I began to see the world differently.

I also realized this was nothing new. While I was in the USAF boot camp training, as a young nineteen-year-old, I remember the technical instructor would teach us what I know now to be a specific type of meditation. I remember it clear as day and often questioned why the US military would teach their soldiers to pray but it was not prayer it was a method scientifically proven to calm the nervous system down. Upon further review of those memories, I realize they were giving us the same techniques I teach now.

Over the last 25 years, I have attended many leadership conferences and spiritual retreats on a quest to heal a part of me that I believed was flawed, broken, and even numb. Of course, in hindsight, I never told myself this was the reason for attending so many conferences and reading so many books but looking back this was the reason. It is clear to me now, that I was trying to fix myself hoping that if I was not broken, then maybe someone would love me and not care that I secretly yearned for a simple hug or for someone to tell me everything would be ok. This is typical behavior of children of alcoholics and children who grew up with traumatic childhoods as I did. After reading hundreds of books and spending thousands of dollars on personal and professional development seminars I can tell you, no one really needs any of it.

You do not need to read another book not even this one or get another course online or attend another spiritual retreat to feel you are more spiritual, smarter, or more deserving than you were last week but rather pause for a minute and feel into this moment (read this sentence again). Life is made up of a series of moments and it is our job to bask in the opportunity to bathe in those moments by tapping into appreciation and joyfulness. That's it. Books and conferences will never give you that. Take this from me, I am the queen of writing books and paying high-ticket coaches to teach me what my heart has known all along. I am love, made by love, and human means being superhuman. Our present realities are our superpower. Our power is held in this very moment and this moment as you read this WORD. This moment is the point of entry to access this power.

By power I don't mean some crazy western idea of control but rather the power to understand the profound depths of our breath, the miracle of our lives and the beauty of our human spirit. I am hesitating as I'm writing this story, but I will share it anyway. This book was inspired by an Instagram post. I know crazy but it's true. It was an old clip of Bob Marley when a reporter asked him if he was a rich man. Bob Marley responded with a confused look and asked, "what do you mean rich?" the reporter then said "you know possessions and things, cars houses, do you own anything" then Bod Marley says "this is what you think rich is? ... I don't have those things my richness is life... I have life". This Instagram post was only a few seconds, but Bob Marley's words 42 years ago penetrated my spirit so deeply that here I am writing this book for you.

Yes **YOU**, I may not know who you are or what miracles life has in store for you, but I know this book and its simple stories may help reveal newfound insight that may propel you to get to the next level in your life. You see I know one thing for sure, without any doubt, life is more mystical than you may believe. In fact, it is so mystical that the very act of you picking up this book and reading this sentence is no accident. I have learned that if we pay attention with intention, we can see what most people ignore. Most people ignore the little voice inside their chest coming from inside their heart that is always telling them what is true.

How is it possible that in less than a few seconds words from 42 years ago from a man that is now dead from melanoma at the age of 36 penetrated me so deeply and vastly that I had to rush to my computer and write this book in two weeks? It is nothing short of the most mystical thing any human can experience. I know this to be true because, under the tutelage of my esteemed Qi Gong teacher, JC Cox, I have come to appreciate the ancient Chinese practice of cultivating vital energy. What I learned from this practice helped me understand how my energy moves throughout my body but also the universe. At the core of this practice lies a profound understanding of the heart's dual significance, both in terms of its physical and energetic manifestations. According to the Qi Gong system, the heart serves as the very seat of consciousness, regulating emotions and governing the mind. The key here is that thousands of years ago our most ancient human traditions understood that the heart and its emotions govern the mind. (Cox, 2023)

Interestingly, in the Qi Gong philosophy, the heart is also believed to be capable of providing unfiltered, non-judgmental answers to our most pressing questions. However, in order to tap into this fountain of wisdom, we must first train our bodies to listen. With now a clearer understanding I believe I died back in May 2021 because I had stopped listening to my heart and my spirit had no communion with it and had nowhere else to go but to ascend to a higher realm of understanding. And because my children still needed me here on earth I returned if only to keep writing about what I know to be true for all humans on the planet. So, I am here writing this book.

My personal journey with my Qi Gong practice began several years before my near-death experience, as I endeavored to broaden my understanding of Eastern philosophy.

Having grown up in a traditional Christian environment, the concepts of chakras, energy lines, and medicinal herbs were initially foreign and difficult to understand. Nonetheless, I felt a deep yearning to understand these ancient practices, believing that they offered a more holistic way of viewing the world than the primitive, divisive methods that have been employed for centuries in countries like my own. You see it makes a difference if you were brought up to believe in the mysteries of life or not. It matters if you think a simple phone call from a friend calling you at the precise moment when you were thinking about them is a coincidence or mystical. I chose the latter because I have tested this over and over and coincidences don't exist only signs for you to follow in essence the whispering of the heart's calling. And I say whispers at first because at first it will be whispers and then you will hear the heart talk to you directly, like my heart did to me when it told me I needed to write about this topic, and I needed to share what Bob Marley said 42 years ago. It was right on point with what wealth and happiness really are.

Wealth and happiness are not the accumulation of material things but the understanding that richness is life. Now 15 years ago I would have said, no I don't think so, it's not how I want people to view me. I don't want people to think I am getting my inspiration from an Instagram post, seriously, but here is the thing, this message is much bigger than me and whether you judge me or not that is on you. My job is to share and love the world so much I must express what my heart is expressing to its truest extent and that is true freedom. ***When you arrive at a place in your life that you are more interested in contributing to the world than you are taking from it your entire life energy shifts.*** Somehow the gates of true abundance open and life appears to be magical every day.

In 2019 before the worldwide pandemic, I attended a conference in Albuquerque New Mexico. The conference was called Scientists, Mystics & Sages, the bridge between science and spirituality. The lineup of speakers was as follows: The physicist Dr. Amit Goswami, Dr. Joe Dispenza, author Anita Morjani, Dr. Bruce Lipton, and author Gregg Braden among many others. I mention these speakers line up because for me they are like the modern-day mystics and sages. You see we live in a time in which most people no longer believe in organized religion or hierarchal concepts of control. We live in a world where just about everyone on the planet has access to information and can learn anything they want and do with it what they choose. And in the realm of the mystical, there are people on the planet that have walked a path that has taken them to a point of no return and their only way forward is the mystical path. It is my belief that certain people on the planet today are providing us with information that our hearts must hear in order for us to evolve, only if you are ready to receive this information.

Me, I began this mystical path with Caroline Myss a modern-day Catholic mystic. It was easy for me to gravitate towards her because she came from a traditional Christian view, and I grew up catholic and when it comes to religions it is my favorite out of all world religions. More on why later. Anyways, Caroline Myss wrote a book years ago that helped me understand mystical symbols and archetypes and I have never been the same since. I could say she was the doorway to my mystical experiences in life and her work helped me heal a lot of past traumas and establish new belief systems. This book is called: Anatomy of the Spirit: The Seven Stages of Power and Healing. (Myss, 2023) It's worth the read.

While I was at the conference in New Mexico with all these amazing authors, speakers, and scientists I had a series of coincidences that transpired. At first, I shrugged them off as coincidental. However, after my near-death experience serval years later, I now know they were full blow-out signs from my heart, from above or from whatever place you want to imagine they came from, but they were real. I felt as though the universe was slapping me on the face trying to get my attention, well not slapping me but something a lot gentler (lol) yet I did not adhere to the signs. Primarily because it is very typical for children of alcoholics to "bypass" the alert signals because it is a way for children to stay alive and survive in their environments. And true to form as an adult I carried this survival mechanism with me not even knowing it. This "bypass" mechanism for many adults that grew up in homes where alcoholism was prevalent, and safety was questionable struggle with this type of "bypass" button. I learned about this in the book "When the Body Says No: The Cost of Hidden Stress" by Dr. Gabor Maté. (Mate, 2023) Anyhow, more about the conference.

Attending a conference always presents the opportunity to meet fascinating individuals. I embarked on this journey solo, leaving my children behind with my then-husband. Driving from Las Vegas to New Mexico proved to be a rejuvenating experience. There is something about traversing the desert that exudes tranquility. I secured accommodations through Airbnb, situated across from a school. The conference, slated for a week, would take place at a stunning Hyatt resort, featuring a spacious conference room capable of accommodating over two thousand attendees. Having devoted ample preparation, I was fervently anticipating the forthcoming event.

On the initial day of the conference, as per my usual practice, I situated myself as close to the stage as possible. For an overachiever like me, note-taking is a skill I relish. Once the speakers graced the stage, I became an efficient note-taking machine. In addition to attending the speakers' sessions, I was keenly aware of the individuals I would encounter and the adventures that awaited. It was on the first day that I met a charming young woman in her twenties. Her mother had passed away a few years prior, and we shared lunch and a one-hour walk before the next session. I was reminded of myself at her age. Although she was working for a large financial firm and earning a good income and appeared to have it all, she was struggling to understand why her mother had left earth so abruptly and her departure saddened her deeply. It was clear that she needed comfort, and during our walk, she began to divulge details about her mother, eventually breaking down in tears. She confessed that she had never wept so intensely before, and it felt like her mother was present, compelling me to reassure her that everything would be okay. I intuited that there was a message her mother would want her to know, and I endeavored to convey it. The experience was peculiar, and I felt as though I was tapping into emotions that I had anticipated based on my prior research. Afterward, we strolled back to the next session, both feeling as though something significant had transpired.

Later that afternoon, I met Dr. Alejandra Orozco, a Colombian researcher who was then living in Africa, undertaking vital work with the locals concerning land issues. Dr. Orozco and I subsequently developed a friendship and co-authored books that expound on our shared mystical encounters. Shortly day two arrived and I found myself sitting next to a local woman, Ana Bee Gonzales, who teaches people how to move their bodies through dance to fully express themselves. Dance is something that has always made me happy, however, I had to admit I had lost my ability to tap into this type of energy and had not danced since my wedding. It seemed almost surreal when I verbalized this to her since in my Latino culture dance is how we heal. We sat on the beautiful green lawn during our lunch after an intense session with Dr. Bruce Lipton and as we ate together, she shared her numerous stories on how people can heal many parts of their lives through movement and dance. It made me think of the native traditions and their understanding of the power of such practices. While we were conversing on the topic, I felt a massive burn on my wedding ring finger and when I took off my wedding band there was a blister of some kind as if my wedding ring had gotten so hot that it burned my skin so severely, I could not put it back on.

I looked over at Ana Bee and we both sat there quietly knowing my body was trying to tell me something. At that moment I completely ignored what my heart was telling me and looked the other way. I knew my marriage was on the brink of dissolving and that I was not happy in the environment in which I lived. At that moment I chose to ignore what my heart and my body were telling me, and I pretended it was just a mere coincidence that my wedding band burned my finger at that moment for no apparent reason while all my other jewelry was intact under the same hot sun.

The conference continued to show me many other coincidences and I would say some miracles and some I chose to acknowledge and some to ignore because of my fear of believing my heart and what truth it was sharing with me. Every single one of the speakers on stage in the conference left an impactful dent in my understanding of this world we call reality. Sometimes we are ready to see the small signs life shows us to guide us in the right direction and other times knowingly we choose to ignore them as I did with my burned finger. Regardless, your journey is your own and everything is divine timing. It does not matter if you choose or don't choose what matters is that you know no matter what you choose, you are infinitely loved and that is the truth.

I have stayed connected with a lot of the people I met at that conference in fact two of the women I mentioned I have authored books with and for that I am grateful. I knew years earlier my marriage would end but I had to literally die to get my final sign that a new life waited for me and that it would be a life that would look much different than the one I had built with my mind and hard work. My new life would be built with my heart and my heart's intention by feeling so much love in my heart that my life would unfold with joy and ease, and I would never recognize it as work but rather a better life than anything I could have ever imagined. Now connecting the dots looking back I can see that it was all meant to be and that it was all done with divine beautiful purpose. I don't' regret any moments or decisions because they were uniquely my own and I love that version of myself as much as I love the new version of myself.

It is no secret that language and the words we use are as powerful as magic. Language is not a toy or a tool to be relegated to the faint of heart. In fact, the knowledge and ancient wisdom of the heart has been known by humanity for thousands of years. In many ways our own language has left us clues as to just how important and mystical the human heart is, for example here are the most common phrases we use in the English language of which people use day in and day out as if it was simply just and expression. I've always wondered how it was we came to these conclusions so much so that we use these expressions without second thought. **Here are some examples:**

"Heart and soul"
"Bare your heart"
"Cold-hearted"
"Cross my heart"
"Follow your heart"
"Have a change of heart"
"Heart of gold"
"Heart-to-heart"
"My heart goes out to you"
"Open-hearted"
"Pierced my heart"
"Set your heart on something"
"Stole my heart"
"Take heart"
"To your heart's content"
"True to heart"
"Wear your heart on your sleeve"
"Weigh heavy on my heart"
"With all my heart"
"You have my heart"

And the list goes on. In my personal experience when it comes to heart expressions, I know hundreds more. In Spanish, the use of the word heart is embedded in the very fabric of the Latino culture. Just imagine all the other world languages. It is my belief that this is the reason why the Latino culture is so passionate about living a life of celebration and honoring our ancestors in particular "el dia de los Muertos" in Mexico. Being bilingual has opened double the doors for me and has been the reason I have thrived in any career I have manifested for myself. Not because I'm smarter but simply because I have access to more words and two languages that allow me to gain a broader perspective of the world around me. This has given me the insight to press on in life when most people would give up and to stay persistent regardless of setbacks. In Spanish these are some of the expressions commonly used:

De todo corazón - "With all my heart"

Tener un corazón de piedra - "To have a heart of stone"

Abrir el corazón- "To open one's heart"

Latir del corazón - "Heartbeat"

Poner el corazón en algo - "To put your heart into something"

Me late el corazón - "My heart beats for you"

No tener corazón - "To have no heart"

Partir el corazón - "To break someone's heart"

Llenar el corazón - "To fill one's heart"

Tener el corazón contento - "To have a happy heart"

Estar con el corazón en la mano - "To have your heart in your hand"

Dejar el corazón en algo - "To leave your heart in something"

Tener un gran corazón - "To have a big heart"
Latir de emoción - "Heart pounding with excitement"
No caber en el corazón - "To be too much to handle emotionally"
Tener el corazón roto - "To have a broken heart"
Dejar el corazón - "To give your all"
Perder el corazón - "To lose one's heart"
Seguir tu corazón - "To follow your heart"

And the list goes on...

The planet's oldest spiritual traditions also have much to say about the heart, **here are some examples:**

Hinduism
"Hridaya" or "Anahata" which refers to the heart chakra, the center of spiritual power in the body.

"Bhakti" or "devotion" which emphasizes the importance of connecting with the divine through the heart and cultivating love and compassion for all beings.

Buddhism
"Karuna" or "compassion" which is seen as the highest virtue in Buddhism and involves cultivating an open heart and a deep sense of empathy for all beings.

"Metta" or "loving-kindness" which involves cultivating a warm and open heart towards oneself and others and is seen as an essential part of the path to enlightenment.

Judaism
"Lev" or "heart" which is seen as the seat of the soul and the source of human emotion and desire.
"Teshuvah" or "repentance" which involves turning the heart towards God and seeking forgiveness for one's transgressions.

Islam
"Qalb" or "heart" which is seen as the center of human consciousness and the seat of faith and belief.

"Taqwa" or "God-consciousness" which involves guarding the heart from impure thoughts and cultivating a deep sense of reverence and awe for God.

Taoism
"Xin" or "heart-mind" which is seen as the source of all human thought and emotion, and the key to spiritual awakening.

"Wu Wei" or "effortless action" which involves acting in harmony with the natural flow of the universe and cultivating a sense of openness and receptivity in the heart.

Confucianism
"Xin" or "heart-mind" which is seen as the source of moral reasoning and ethical conduct.
"Ren" or "benevolence" which involves cultivating a loving and compassionate heart towards all beings and is seen as the highest virtue in Confucianism.

Zoroastrianism

"Dil" or "heart" which is seen as the seat of human consciousness and the source of moral reasoning and ethical conduct.

"Humata, Hukhta, Huvarshta" or "good thoughts, good words, good deeds" which involves cultivating a pure, loving heart, and living a life of virtue and service to others.

Shinto

"Kokoro" or "heart" which is seen as the source of human emotion and the connection to the divine.
"Misogi" or "purification" which involves cleansing the heart and the body of impurities and connecting with the pure and natural world.

Jainism

"Hridaya" or "heart" which is seen as the source of all human emotion and the key to spiritual awakening.
"Ahimsa" or "non-violence" which involves cultivating a compassionate and loving heart towards all beings and abstaining from harm and violence.

Sikhism

"Hirda" or "heart" which is seen as the center of spiritual power and the connection to the divine.
"Seva" or "selfless service" which involves cultivating a loving and compassionate heart and serving others with humility and devotion.

As I conclude this chapter, I am left with a sense of wonder and gratitude for the mystical heart and the wisdom keepers who have shared their knowledge with me. Through my personal journey, I have come to understand that the heart is not just a physical organ but a profound source of intuition and wisdom that can guide us in our lives. By connecting with our hearts and learning to listen to its whispers, we can tap into a realm of understanding that is beyond our linear comprehension. The mystical heart has the power to lead us to our true path, to heal our traumas, and to help us unlock our full potential.

Through my work as a HeartMath Coach and my encounters with mystical practitioners, I have realized that there is much more to this world than what meets the eye. There is an unseen realm, an energetic field that interconnects us all, and that can provide us with the answers we seek if we learn to listen. We are not merely physical beings, but we are also spiritual beings having a human experience, and the mystical heart is the gateway to our spiritual essence.

As we move through life, we are presented with a series of moments that can shape our destiny. It is up to us to pay attention to the signs and listen to the whispers of our hearts. Through the mystical heart, we can tap into a deeper understanding of our breath, the miracle of our lives, and the beauty of our human spirit. Our present realities are our superpowers, and by living in the present moment, we can access the full power of our hearts.

Upon returning home from the wonderful conference in New Mexico, I eagerly began implementing the valuable insights I had gained and became a whirlwind of activity. However, in the midst of my busyness, I lost sight of the very reason I had pursued this newfound wisdom - to connect with my heart and follow its intuitive guidance. I soon realized my mistake and organized a successful spiritual conference of my own. From my experience, I can attest that it's easy to become so engrossed in appearing spiritual that we forget our true nature as spiritual beings. We don't need to do anything or go anywhere to embrace this truth - it resides within us. We simply need to allow ourselves to be. It may seem challenging, but it's worth it.

For many years, I believed that being busy and achieving tangible accomplishments were the keys to gaining access to some elusive spiritual club, and the rewards that come with it. In a society like ours, which thrives on recognition and achievement, this mindset is all too common. However, I've learned that paying attention to the heart is paramount, and the daily practice of heartfulness can be transformative. It's a small but powerful act that has the potential to change your life forever.

Chapter 5

Aligning with the Heart:
Attracting Your Hearts Desires

Healing is a matter of time, but it is sometimes also a matter of opportunity.
~Hippocrates

Once I grasped the language necessary to communicate with my heart, aligning with it became a breeze. Unfortunately, this language isn't typically taught in school or even in church. However, once you understand how to connect and align with your heart, attracting and manifesting your desires becomes second nature. I used to be skeptical of the spiritual jargon so prevalent in Western society. In fact, I made a promise to myself to never use words like "spiritual," "god-fearing," or "mystical."

As I delved deeper into my spiritual practice and gained a better understanding of myself as a spiritual being, I worried that I had merely traded one organized religion for another. However, that wasn't the case. All I had to do was comprehend my emotions and perspective on the world and within myself. This allowed me to focus on my intention behind the words rather than judging the words themselves. It was that simple.

Initially, the new spiritual terminology I encountered seemed like something out of a sci-fi novel. Words like "astral projection," "akashic records," "dimensions," and "spiritual guides" struck me as absurd. When my spiritual coach, Lee Papa, informed me that I had broken through a spiritual veil and entered another dimension, I couldn't help but roll my eyes in disbelief and pass judgment on her comprehension of my situation. Looking back, I'm grateful that she took me on as a client despite my rebelliousness toward her teachings. In retrospect, what occurred after I embraced this newfound knowledge was nothing short of miraculous. I realized that criticizing this unfamiliar jargon would get me nowhere. Instead, I needed to remain patient and observe what unfolded before me.

So, I sat and listened attentively. Ironically, it was someone from the church I attended who gave me a book by Gregg Braden. The insights in that book led me to abandon my pursuit of a theology certification at a Christian bible college. My friends from church thought I was losing my mind, as I had been so focused on saving people from eternal damnation that I lost sight of why I believed in the first place. I concluded that belief was unnecessary - all I needed was to reflect quietly on my heart's desires and observe how life magically unfolds. I also discovered that learning the truth can transform you and set you free in every aspect of your life. As someone who has always valued coaching and mentorship, I continued to learn, but this time on my own terms. I sought out people like Lee Papa and others who offered fresh perspectives on spirituality and provided the language I needed to articulate the message my heart had been yearning to convey for years.

As one of my bible college professors, the late Dr. Shaw, used to advise, "Explore as many religions as possible and form your own conclusions." I miss Dr. Shaw dearly, as he imparted invaluable wisdom and knowledge to me. When we first met, I was delighted to discover that he had been mentored by Mother Teresa of Calcutta, despite his current position at a Protestant college that didn't necessarily endorse the Catholic faith. This taught me that unexpected people and situations can teach us valuable lessons, and that the key is to remain open to learning, leaving the rest to our hearts to discern. Eventually, I left that Christian bible college and became a seeker of truth, or, in the words of Caroline Myss, a "mystic without a monastery."

At the core of my quest for knowledge was my desire to manifest the best version of myself. Initially, I sought material wealth and possessions. However, as I delved deeper into my heart, my desires shifted toward freedom from suffering, feelings of joy, and emotions of peace. I realized that what I thought I wanted was not aligned with what I truly desired - society had merely imposed its ideals upon me. So, how does one practically align with their heart?

Here are some examples of what I did to reconnect and in other terms, plug into my heart again:

Talk to your heart as if it were a person: with your right or left hand tap the middle of your chest and then practice these examples:

Spend time in nature to get in touch with the beauty and stillness that surrounds you. This practice is my favorite because I know my healing was directly correlated to the time I spent out in nature. It seems so cliché that hugging a tree solved my health issues, but it was more than that. Being out in nature reminded me of who I am and why I am here on earth and that is only something the human heart can understand.

Embrace vulnerability and authenticity, allowing yourself to express your true feelings and desires, without fear of judgment. When you judge something or someone (aka) yourself it becomes "sticky" so simply observe when you feel like crying don't judge it, just do it.

Practice self-reflection to identify patterns and behaviors that may be holding you back, and to cultivate self-awareness. Self-reflection and self-awareness are not judgement, it is simply observing. Remember to be kind when you do this and go to the heart directly: example: So, heart, what do I need to know?

Keep a journal to record your thoughts, feelings, and desires, and to reflect on your journey towards alignment with the heart. In particular, the space between "sleep and awake" which many sleep and dream experts call the hypnogogic state. This is the space between sleep and awake in which Robert Moss, the author of "The history of dreams" says is the space when we have a window to make magic happen. I've tried this for many years, and it is truly a magical place to be so much, so I'll be writing about this in my following book.

Practice appreciation by focusing on the positive aspects of your life and expressing appreciation for what you have. Sometimes it seemed so hard for me to focus on the positive especially during a lengthy litigation process during my divorce. What I did to mitigate my dilemma was that I would write down 20 things to appreciate and read them aloud to myself until my heart would feel them. Soon I was on my way to appreciating everything and everyone around me.

Engage in acts of kindness and service to others, which can promote feelings of connection and purpose. There is something you can do to help someone that you know can never repay you back and that is why we must do this. Being kind and of service is a selfish act in many ways because the giver reaps the benefit even more than the person who receives.

Spend time with loved ones who uplift and support you, and who share your values and interests.
Practice breathing exercises to calm your mind and focus your attention on the present moment and in the area of

the heart. Talk to your heart and say, "I understand" "All is well".

The heart is a powerful force that exists within each and every one of us. When we align ourselves with our heart's true desires, we can attract abundance, joy, and fulfillment into our lives. Wealth and happiness are the results of you listening to your heart at such a deep level that you begin to understand that wealth and happiness are already a part of who you are. In other words, waiting for something to happen is not part of the equation. It's already happening, you just need to tune-in to it.

Aligning with the heart is not just about listening to its voice - it is also about taking action. We must be willing to follow the guidance of the heart and take steps toward our deepest desires. This means taking risks, stepping out of our comfort zone, and trusting in the wisdom of the heart. When we align our actions with the desires of the heart, we can manifest our heart's desires into reality. Case in point me writing this book was and is all about acting on what my heart, not my head, was guiding me to do, for unknown reasons to me other than I understand that when the heart speaks you listen and take action. Now keep in mind, yes, I still have other things to do like my taxes, the rearing of my children and laundry but for now this urgent call from my heart to pen these words and crystalize them on paper is a bit more important at least for the next couple of days until publication.

So, how do we attract our heart's desires? One of the key principles of manifestation is the law of attraction, which states that like attracts like. This means that we attract into our lives what we focus our attention on.

When we focus on positive thoughts and emotions, we attract positive experiences and opportunities. Conversely, when we focus on negative thoughts and emotions, we attract negativity into our lives. Now, this is only one side of the story, the other side is that you must FEEL your heart and emote these emotions for the law of attraction to really work. The law of attraction has gotten a lot of attention in the last ten years, however what most people don't know is that there are hundreds of universal laws that are also at play that can help you manifest. It is my belief that whatever laws help you tap into your heart and help you connect with your heart are the ones you must pay close attention to.

Law of Vibration: Everything in the universe vibrates at a certain frequency, including our thoughts and emotions. By aligning our vibrations with what we desire, we can attract it into our lives.

Law of Correspondence: As above, so below. This law states that the patterns and structures in the universe are reflected on every scale, from the smallest to the largest.

Law of Gestation: Every seed that is planted takes time to germinate and grow, and so do our ideas and desires.

We must be patient and give them the time they need to manifest.

Law of Polarity: Everything has two opposite poles, such as good and evil, light, and dark. By recognizing and embracing both sides of a polarity, we can find balance and harmony.

Law of Rhythm: Everything in the universe moves in cycles and patterns, from the tides to the seasons. By understanding and working with these rhythms, we can achieve greater success and happiness.

Law of Gender: Everything in the universe has masculine and feminine aspects, including our thoughts and emotions. By balancing these aspects within ourselves, we can achieve greater wholeness and creativity.

Law of Cause and Effect: Every action has a corresponding reaction, and every cause has an effect. By being aware of the effects we create, we can take responsibility for our actions and create more positive outcomes.

Law of Compensation: The universe rewards us according to the value we bring to others. By focusing on providing value and service, we can attract greater abundance and success.

Law of Non-Resistance: By letting go of resistance and attachment, we can flow with the universe and achieve greater ease and success.

Law of Forgiveness: Forgiveness is essential for releasing negative energy and moving forward in life. By forgiving others and ourselves, we can create greater peace and healing.

Law of Unity: Everything in the universe is interconnected and part of a larger whole. By recognizing our oneness with all things, we can create greater harmony and cooperation.

Law of Reflection: Everything we see in others is a reflection of something within ourselves. By using these reflections as opportunities for growth and healing, we can transform ourselves and our relationships.

Law of Surrender: By surrendering our attachment to outcomes and trusting in the universe, we can achieve greater peace and fulfillment.

Law of Action: While the universe responds to our thoughts and intentions, we must also take action in the physical world to create the results we desire.

Law of Perpetual Transmutation: Energy is constantly flowing and transforming, and we can direct this energy through our thoughts and intentions to manifest our desires.

Law of Attraction for Opposites: This law states that sometimes we attract the opposite of what we think we want in order to learn important lessons or make necessary changes.

Law of Intention and Desire: By setting clear intentions and aligning our desires with our higher purpose, we can manifest our dreams more easily.

Law of Alignment: When our thoughts, emotions, and actions are aligned with our desires, we can achieve greater success and fulfillment.

Law of Gratitude: By focusing on gratitude for what we have, we can attract more abundance and joy into our lives.

Law of Trust: By trusting in the universe and ourselves, we can overcome fear and achieve our goals with greater ease and confidence.

Therefore, in order to attract our heart's desires, we must first cultivate a positive mindset and an attitude of appreciation. This means focusing on what we have rather than what we lack and approaching life with a sense of optimism and hope. When we cultivate a positive mindset, we create a vibrational frequency that is aligned with our heart's desires, and we attract positive experiences and opportunities into our lives. However, cultivating a positive mindset is not enough on its own.

We must also **take action** towards our *heart's desires*. This means setting clear goals and taking steps towards achieving them. We must be willing to take risks, overcome obstacles, and trust in the guidance of the heart. When we align with the heart and act towards our desires, we begin to attract abundance, joy, and fulfillment into our lives. This is because the heart is connected to a force that is greater than us - the universal energy of love and abundance. When we align with this energy, we tap into a source of infinite possibility and potential. We become co-creators of our reality, and we can manifest our heart's desires into reality.

It is important to note that aligning with the heart is not just about manifesting our external desires. It is also about connecting with our inner selves and living a life that is true to our deepest values and beliefs. When we align with the heart, we tap into a sense of purpose and meaning that goes beyond material success or achievement.

Furthermore, aligning with the heart is not a one-time event. It is an ongoing process of self-discovery and self-awareness. We must constantly check-in with ourselves and make sure that we are still aligned with our heart's desires. This means being willing to let go of old patterns and beliefs that no longer serve us and being open to new possibilities and experiences. In order to truly align with the heart, we must also cultivate a sense of compassion and love towards ourselves. This means being gentle and kind to ourselves, and treating ourselves with the same care and concern that we would offer to others. When we learn to love and accept ourselves, we create a space of inner peace and wholeness that allows us to connect with our deepest desires.

Additionally, if we look back far enough, we find that at the center of manifesting our realities our most ancient traditions understood the heart was and is at the core of everything and through its wisdom we can manifest.

For example, in ancient Egypt, the heart was believed to be the center of a person's being and the source of their thoughts and feelings. The heart was also believed to be the seat of the soul and was therefore considered to be the most important organ. The ancient Egyptians believed that after death, the heart would be weighed against the feather of Ma'at, the goddess of truth and justice, and if the heart was found to be pure and free from sin, the person's soul would be allowed to enter the afterlife. Now I don't know about you, but they took the idea of the heart being the center of our lives pretty seriously.

In Hinduism, the heart is considered to be the center of spiritual and emotional intelligence. It is believed that the heart is the seat of the soul and that it is through the heart that we connect with the divine. Protecting the heart means cultivating qualities such as compassion, kindness, and love, which are considered essential for spiritual growth and enlightenment. And as mentioned in previous chapters in Taoism, the heart is seen as the seat of the spirit and the source of wisdom and intuition. Taoist teachings emphasize the importance of keeping the heart clear and uncluttered so that it can be receptive to the wisdom of the universe. This involves cultivating a calm and peaceful mind, and avoiding negative emotions such as anger, fear, and anxiety.

In Buddhism, the heart is seen as the source of all suffering and the key to liberation. Buddhist teachings emphasize the importance of cultivating a compassionate and loving heart, and of practicing mindfulness and awareness in order to overcome negative emotions and mental states. In all these traditions, protecting the heart means cultivating positive qualities such as compassion, kindness, and love, while avoiding negative emotions and mental states that can lead to suffering and hinder spiritual growth.

So, how do you align with the Heart and attract your heart's desires: learn the laws of nature, use the tools available to you in this book. And above all, pay attention to your heart's intentions, which is the center of everything you do. Talk to your heart as if it were a person and become friends with it just like you would an old friend. Spend time in nature and ask your heart to guide you. It is far from a fairytale method of manifestation but one that is now being proven to be real and one that our most ancient wisdom keepers have known all along. The key is to focus on the area of the heart, touch it with you hand or your mind's eye and pretend it is speaking back at you.

Now, I am off to manifest the next chapter of this book.

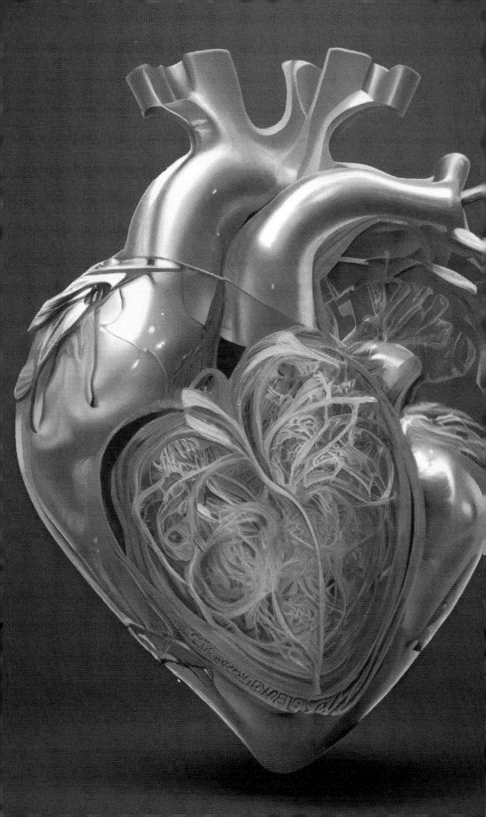

Chapter 6

Listening to the Wisdom Within: Heart's Rhythms

If you listen long enough, the patient will give you the diagnosis.
~Sir William Osler

In this world, there exist two distinct categories of individuals: those who harbor an unshakeable conviction that they were brought into existence for a specific purpose, and those who do not. The differentiation between these two groups can become hazy when we are confronted with the squalor and chaos of life. The truth is, existence can be messy and, at times, grossly unjust and unfair.

Nevertheless, none of us can deny the incredible potency of love and the vigor of the energy that courses through our hearts. It is this force that makes the experience of enduring and surviving the madness of the world worth the effort, regardless of how arduous it may be. In my personal opinion, a truly fulfilling life would involve leaving the world in a better condition than when I first arrived. I strongly believe that this would give my life purpose and meaning, and I hope to achieve this before my time comes.

As I learned to attune to the wisdom of my heart and listen to its counsel, I felt as though my life had been finally unshackled. Though such moments of liberation were scarce in my life, each instance when I elected to embrace love over fear is etched in my memory. For example: as a young girl growing up in an abusive household and enduring the toxic legacy of parental alcoholism, the odds of achieving personal success were dim. Indeed, for children of alcoholics, if we do prevail, it is often only through the aid of understanding the power of the heart and its pull to love. The devastation created by early-life maltreatment may take years to restore. Western physicians refer to those of us who suffer from such circumstances as ACEs, denoting Adverse Childhood Experiences: a term which encompasses the traumas of abuse, neglect, and domestic dysfunction, and the enduring impact on health and well-being. As for myself, I not only bear the mark of ACE, but also the scar of severe PTSD incurred during my military service.

My life has been a tumultuous ebb and flow: periods of serenity mingled with seasons of agony so acute I wish they had never been. Yet, through some kind of divine agency, I was guided and anchored to my course. By "guided," I do not mean an otherworldly voice commanding me, but rather a fervent conviction within me, within my heart, that whispered: "You are loved, and you are love. Life will become better, keep going, tomorrow will be better."

It was not my religious upbringing nor my years of theological study that opened my eyes to the beauty of life, but rather the kindness and empathy extended to me by teachers, mentors, neighbors, friends, and every dog that has graced my path. I have spent my lifetime unraveling the realization that life is an amalgam of moments, and in each moment lies a choice. The choice to embrace love and compassion, or to let busyness shackle our ability to recognize the opportunities that are present in each moment. It is the choice to listen to the heart, as our ancient spiritual traditions hold that the heart's wisdom is higher than the laws of men or organized religion.

The highs and lows of my life have become the simple rhythm of existence. There are defining moments that shape us and moments that challenge us, and in each instance, if we pause to consult the heart, it will guide us. However, we must approach each decision from a place of love, rather than fear. The difference between the two is palpable, as one choice brings us closer to peace, while the other unleashes chaos in the world. I know this to be true, for I have made a series of choices that have defined my destiny. Though I harbor no regrets, many of these choices have made my life far more difficult than necessary.

My earliest memory of a defining moment occurred when I was a mere five years of age. Witnessing my father sinking into the abyss of alcoholism, I swore an oath to myself that I would never drink. This was followed by another momentous decision when, after two years of college, I convinced myself that poor children were not meant to earn degrees, especially not in music, and abandoned my studies to enlist in the United States Air Force. Though the military proved an adventure, it was not a path aligned with the yearnings of my heart. It was during my service in the military that I encountered a man whom I loved so much and altered the trajectory of my existence, but my fear led me to flee our commitment to each other and opt for a different path. The years that followed were full of choices made from a place of fear, rather than love. I would choose one course over another because it was safer or do things to please others regardless of my own needs and heart's desires.

I chased after prestigious corporate titles, acquiring them only to discover that true leadership transcends titles and centers on service to others. The times when I followed the urgings of my heart were often arduous and fraught with pain but ultimately proved more rewarding and fruitful. I recognize that pursuing one's heart's calling can be intimidating and necessitate difficult choices, such as relinquishing friendships or abandoning careers that no longer align with one's life purpose. But the reward for taking such leaps of faith is profound. We unavoidably revert to our most authentic self, characterized by love, compassion, and heartfulness.

I have been blessed with a series of deep and loving relationships, none of which proved enduring, but all of which left me feeling enriched, for I had allowed my heart to lead the way. Pain, while often unwelcome, is a vital ingredient for living life to the fullest. Only through experiencing the full breadth and depth of our emotions can we truly appreciate the richness of love and the generosity of the human heart.

In all my years, I have learned that one can never err by choosing love. The blessings that have graced my life are a testament to the enduring power of this force, for I have chosen love over fear more often than the other way around.

Never doubt that the heart inside your chest is speaking to you at every moment. It speaks to you in between every breath and in your dreams. It may come as a silent reminder of how much you are loved and how your potential to be love and give love is more powerful than anything else you will ever possess. In life, something will crush you so hard that you may feel lost and incapable of loving again or caring about the world again, but you must remember you are not your thoughts. Your thoughts do not define you. You define yourself. Your heart is you speaking because the heart is the seat of the soul, and you are a soul before you are anything else. Never doubt this.

Tuning into the heart's whispers and wisdom can prove a grueling undertaking, as the voice may initially seem too faint to be heard. But I implore you not to abandon the pursuit, for when one focuses and listens attentively, the whispers emerge. The heart's urgings manifest in diverse forms, as they did for me.

For example, my beloved boxer, Gracie, would place her paw on my lap every time I sat down to dinner, and I would swat her away, irritated by her persistence. For months, she repeated this ritual, but I never heeded her subtle petitions. Then one day, she died on my kitchen floor, and I raced downstairs to comfort my hysterical children. As I cradled her lifeless body and lamented the fact that she had left us too soon, I could not shake the thought of that memory for months, Gracie had been attempting to convey something to me at the dinner table. It was unusual behavior for her, and this is why I sense that it was an extraordinary effort to catch my attention. The profound sorrow that overtook me proved too much to bear, and within two weeks, I had a near-death experience. I am not asserting that I perished from grief, but rather that our animals play a pivotal role in how we communicate with ourselves. Animals have other methods of communicating with one another, and I have no doubt that Gracie was endeavoring to inform me of some illness in my body. However, I did not listen to her signals, for I lacked compassion for my dear sweet friend. Each evening, during dinner, Gracie presented me with an opportunity to connect with my heart and hers, yet I opted instead to feel irritated, tired, and annoyed by her ceaseless demands for attention. In each of those moments, I made a choice, electing annoyance over love. It is as straightforward as that.

Every moment presents a choice, and we must choose wisely. I do not blame myself for Gracie's death, nor do I lament the missed opportunities, for I am grateful for the time we shared and the love and joy that was shared in our relationship. That is sufficient for me, and I know it was for her. That moment of Gracie's death reminded me of how many times in my life I was being guided by my heart to pay attention to listen more carefully but on many occasions, I was simply too tired or too irritated or felt it would be too much work and so I settled knowing in the long run, they were not my heart's desires but it was easier to stay at that job or in that relationship.

I cherish the knowledge that those days of indecision and uncertainty I have relegated to the past. Armed with an abundance of courage, I have embarked upon a trajectory dictated by the urgings of my heart in recent years. Despite my countless experiences, I consider my life to be a wondrous adventure, for love invariably triumphs over fear, and it is in these moments of love that life reveals its greatest wonders. There exist no mistakes in life, merely experiences that push us toward the next level of evolution. There are no right or wrong choices, only choices. Whatever decision one arrives at, one must approach oneself with kindness and bless oneself, for, in the end, love reigns supreme, and each of us is inherently imbued with love. You will always be loved, and your heart attests to this with each pulse and every breath. Never forget this.

My dear Gracie loved me so much and I still feel her love every day. My father although he suffered and struggled with his own demons, he was a man that loved me. I know this to be true because I could feel it inside my chest and I knew deep down in my heart he yearns to understand the language of love, but he was overruled by his logical mind not being able to make that long journey from his head to his heart. That is the longest journey anyone will ever make.

The potent expression of love derives from the center of your chest, do not ignore it, and do not run from it. For, this is the most exquisite more empowering emotion you will ever experience in this life. It is worth every mistake and every painful moment because when you can truly connect with your heart and listen to its voice and heed its song you will be changed forever. In this world, there exist two distinct categories of individuals: those who harbor an unshakeable conviction that they were brought into existence for a specific purpose, and those who do not, so, which one are you?

Chapter 7

Heartful Fulfillment:
Simplicity and Mentorship

"The more simple we are, the more complete we become."
~ Auguste Rodin

In the realm of spirituality, there is a notion that certain actions or behaviors are necessary to achieve a higher state of being. It is believed that one must sit for hours in the darkness, lighting candles and praying fervently in order to attain enlightenment, contorting one's body into positions that border on the impossible, until all feeling is lost. This is no exaggeration, as I can attest, having been a devout "prayer warrior" who would offer up prayers for strangers and the world at large with an almost desperate fervor, convinced that the fate of the world rested solely on my shoulders. But I had been misguided, as so many of us are. We let the rigidity of man's ideas corrupt the purity and simplicity of our hearts, which is the essence of spirituality. You can be spiritual, wealthy, and happy without damming the world if they don't believe what you believe.

I am eternally grateful for my Christian upbringing and faith, but I had to learn that true spirituality lies in loving oneself first. Every time I chose to walk away from a situation or relationship that did not align with my heart's desires, I was loving myself. Every time I said no to a request that would have compromised my moral integrity or violated my sense of self, I was taking a step closer to understanding what true happiness and wealth truly are.

We make the concept of being human and understanding ourselves far too complicated. We get lost in the rhetoric of religious and spiritual terminology, and we forget the essence of what it means to be spiritual. It is not necessary to kneel before an altar and plead for mercy or wear symbols to proclaim our enlightenment. We can pray or meditate while doing simple tasks such as washing dishes, driving a car, or tending to our plants. By tapping into the presence of our hearts, we can make these everyday activities into sacred rituals and habits, performed with great heartfulness and awareness.

Following my near-death experience, I realized that I had let my prayer life fall by the wayside for over a year. I had not been paying attention to my heart and had allowed toxicity and dysfunction to enter my family life. I had ignored the signals my heart was sending me, including those from my beloved dog, Gracie. Prayer, in essence, is the language of the heart, and it is not about making requests or demanding things from the heart. It is about meditating on the beauty of the present moment and being grateful for the opportunity to live and breathe in it. There is no sweeter sound to the heart than the soul recognizing the beauty of this moment, free of judgment and filled with appreciation for life. It's simple to live in this moment, whether one is washing clothes, driving kids to school, or cleaning the house. There is no need to kneel before an altar or sit in front of a holy book, reciting scripture, unless that is what speaks to one's heart. I do have a small table in my room with beautiful rocks and deities and incense (don't judge me) however they are not necessarily at all in fact none of it is. For me these things are simply a reminder to my heart to pause during the day and soak in the wonder of being alive one more day.

During my year of recovery, as I reconnected with my heart and regained my sense of self, I realized that heartfulness is easy. We overcomplicate spiritual practices with symbols, rocks, holy objects, spiritual books, seminars, and retreats, distracting ourselves from the simplicity of connecting with our hearts. In fact, one can become so consumed with the minutia of spirituality that life crashes in as a reminder that everything boils down to understanding the concept of "Prioritizing the Heart's Wisdom over Rational Thinking, and Choosing Love over Fear"

When I first realized my connection with my heart was severed, I decided to get back in communication with my heart because I understood this was the only way, I heard the word walk. So, I did. I went walking knowing that was my prayer and my meditation, and with the help of over ten medical doctors and many more spiritual healers and mentors that held my hand while I regained my connection with my heart, it was all as easy as going for a walk. I'm not suggesting you can walk disease away by merely walking every day although depending on your illness it can do better than harm, what I am suggesting is that there is no need to complicate this. Connecting to the heart is about attention with intention and action. I'll also go as far as saying celebrating every milestone is also a key component. Here are more ways you can connect with your heart daily and with more intention for meaningful connection:

Spend time in nature and appreciate the beauty around you to include the mud, the ugly rocks and the old ugly bushes. These observations are all part of it, part of the wholeness of beauty.

Listen to your favorite music and allow it to move your soul and move with that music. Move your body to mirror the sounds.

Practice deep breathing exercises to calm your mind and connect with your body while sitting next to a tree. Pretend the tree is holding your hand. Sound crazy but there is science behind this.

Start a gratitude journal and write down things you are thankful for each day to include the water heater not working or car breaking down. Yes, even those things.

Take up a creative hobby, such as painting or writing, to express yourself. I took my sixteen-year-old son to the gun range to learn how to shoot, something I would have never done ever but I did it anyways because when I tapped into my heart, I knew I would no longer fear guns. It was an unusual thing for me to do but I went with the flow.

Practice forgiveness and let go of grudges and resentments. Ask your heart to bring light to all those people you haven't forgiven yet a make room in your day to send them love and light and all good things.

Connect with loved ones and strengthen your relationships and be specific about the things you will be doing together.

Practice heartfulness and live in the present moment while talking to your heart as if it were a person.

Volunteer and give back to your community or simply reach out to people you know need your help and help them. You may have a skill that someone else could benefit from and you can help by providing your skill set for free.

Take a break from technology and disconnect in order to connect with your heart by going outside.
Engage in physical exercise to release endorphins and boost your mood like weight training.

Eat nourishing foods to fuel your body and mind like veggie smoothies.

Set boundaries and prioritize self-care to honor your needs and desires.

Engage in acts of kindness and spread love to others.

Practice self-reflection and self-awareness to understand yourself better.

Spend time alone and enjoy your own company, get all dressed up just because and dine alone.

Find a spiritual community that resonates with your beliefs and values.

Read spiritual literature and gain insights and inspiration. I would include all the world religions and their spiritual text as they all have wonderful insights to help the human spirit evolve.

Practice visualization and manifest your dreams and goals, in particular study from the work of Robert Monroe and Jose Silva and the work of Dr Brian Weiss. These men have written about how the mind and manifestation work in practical terms, and they also write about the importance understanding the unknowns. They provide tools that I use daily like Robert Monroe binaural beats and Jose Silvas visualization protocols.

Trust your intuition and follow your heart's guidance by practicing heartfulness.

And so many more.

In addition to incorporating many of the practices detailed earlier, I have found solace in the wisdom of Richard Rudd, a new mentor and spiritual guide who appeared in my life during my recovery. His teachings center on the Gene Keys, and his work is dedicated to helping individuals discover their purpose in life, while providing an array of tools to support them along the way. For me, having a mentor is crucial, and I found Rudd's teachings particularly valuable because of his frequent use of the word **"gentle"**.

Throughout my life, I have rarely been gentle with myself, and I sensed that someone like Richard Rudd could teach me this important skill. His unique upbringing resonated with me, and I wholeheartedly recommend seeking out mentors who understand the true essence of wealth and happiness, as well as the pivotal role of the heart in our incredible human existence.

During my visit to Richard Rudd's website,[1] I took a test that provided insight into my personal journey. Though the results were intensely personal, I believe they are worth sharing, particularly as we are all in this together. By sharing who we are and discovering our purpose on this

---

[1] https://genekeys.com/about/

planet through our hearts, we can support one another and create a better world for all. As you've made it this far into the book, I felt it would be helpful to offer these results as an additional tool for you to use on your own journey toward greater fulfillment and self-awareness. Of course, your results would be vastly different from mine but when I read my results, I couldn't believe just how accurate it was in the description of my journey. The insight I gained was invaluable.

(Adriana's)

My Life's Work - what I'm here to do - **Gene Key 45**

You are like the hub of a wheel within your milieu. Whether this be your extended family, business, community, or an even larger arena, you have an extremely important role to play in the world - to act as a focal gathering point for people, ideas, dreams, and enterprises. The people you know in the world are of great importance to you, not for their influence, but because they all have you in common. This opens up all kinds of opportunities for you to offer to the world. The greatest challenge for you will be to let go of your need to be in control. If you can do this, you will release an energy of deep trust into your world that will pull other people's commitment toward you. You carry the genes that would have marked you out as an authority figure within a hierarchy, but you are here to break that ancient pattern of hierarchy. The only way this old pattern can be dissolved is for people like you to make the ultimate act of sovereignty allowing others as much say as you. (Rudd, 2023)

My Evolution - what I'm here to learn - **Gene Key 26**

Your great challenge in life is to harness the power of your own ego. Your ability to speak and communicate with power is the source of your art. You must learn exactly when to flaunt yourself and when to hide yourself. If you get the balance and timing wrong in this, you will end up feeling rejected. You need to see life as though it was a play, and your personality is your costume. You can enhance certain parts of yourself as you need to, but you should never get lost in your role. Above all, you need to communicate a sense of fun to others, even if what you are doing seems serious and important. When you begin to enjoy the many facets of yourself without getting lost in them, you will feel truly free.

My Radiance - what keeps me healthy - **Gene Key 22**

With the 22nd Gene Key in this position, your health and general well-being are entirely connected to your ability to maintain emotional balance. This position is known as the Radiance because it concerns the harmonization of all the various levels of our aura. Your aura is healthy and balanced when your mind is calm. Even though your emotions can swell and swoop, your mind must maintain a detachment from your feelings, as though you were watching yourself from a distance. In this way, you can reap the multitude of gifts that come from your emotional life, as well as avoid the numerous pitfalls. The trick for you is to learn when to be alone and when to be with others. There is an inner light that wants to burn inside you if you can put all your own concerns aside. You have only to forgive yourself and learn to love the life that is yours, and this light will begin to shine out from inside you. At the highest level, you are here to be a beacon of hope and solace for others in times of difficulty.

My Purpose - what deeply fulfills me - **Gene Key 47**

At a mythic level, your purpose is to bring light into places where there is no light. On a mundane level, this means that you must not get stuck with any single way of being. Everything about you is changing all the time, so you had better learn to appreciate this about yourself. You can be consistent, but don't define yourself by your past. You should savor those elements of your past that have brought you to where you are, but the quicker you can let go of the past, the more life will bless you. As you become more aligned with your Purpose, you will see how it constantly changes you, so that it becomes consistent rather than you. Your life will hinge upon a series of sporadic transformations that will completely dismantle your reality, and lead to a whole new cycle each time. Life is not about success or failure for you — it's about turning lead into gold.

Richard Rudd's work is multifaceted and rich, but when I turned to my heart for guidance on whether to share it, the answer was a resounding yes. It is vital that we speak openly about our individual journey and share the expansive nature of our understanding of the world, for it is only through this process that we can help each other evolve. Our human existence is a complex tapestry, but when we simplify it, we can achieve so much more. One way to attain this greater understanding is by seeking out people, resources, and ideas that offer fresh perspectives and resonate with the song in our hearts. It is a never-ending quest, but one that is infinitely rewarding, for it allows us to enjoy this journey of life together, rather than alone. So, let us make it easy, not worrying about the how, when, or with whom, but rather acting on what we feel our hearts are telling us. It need not be a grand breakthrough that is too large to implement; it can be as simple as walking and asking the heart for truth.

It is with the utmost sincerity that I express my deepest hope that the knowledge and insights shared in this book will shower you with blessings and offer a glimpse into the true nature of wealth and genuine happiness as we continue to evolve together. My own journey has taught me that ignoring the whispers of my heart was a mistake, but I also recognize that life moves in seasons, each with its own rhythm. It is my responsibility to attune myself to the music and remain ever cognizant of the vital connection between my heart and mind, so that I may never lose my way again. And if I do, I am reminded to be gentle with myself and to extend love to those around me.

My journey towards my heartfulness practice has been marked by a series of breakthroughs and setbacks. Along the way, I've explored various faiths, left a Christian bible college, and embraced my identity as a truth seeker. Throughout it all, I've been guided by the wisdom of my heart and the whispers of wisdom. The memories of my beloved Gracie and the smiles of my children have provided solace during the darkest moments of my life, and I will forever cherish them.

The numerous teachers, medical professionals, and mentors who have crossed my path have been instrumental in my breakthroughs. However, it is ultimately my heart, and the ancient wisdom that resides within it, that has been my greatest ally and friend. It has guided me towards becoming a fierce and compassionate soul, capable of slaying the dragons that stand in my way to achieving my dreams.

As I continue on this journey, I'm reminded of the power of heartful living and the transformative effect it has had on my life. The wisdom of the heart, passed down through the generations, has led me to become the person I am today - a warrior, a writer, and a spiritual seeker. I hope that my story inspires you to tap into the ancient wisdom of your own heart and the whispers of your ancestors, to embrace your spirituality, and to live a life filled with courage and compassion.

In Summary

Slaying Dragons
with Heartfulness

As I conclude this book, I am filled with a sense of appreciation and hope. Appreciation for the opportunity to share my journey with you and hope that my words have kindled a flame of hope in your heart. I want to use this final chapter to summarize the key lessons I have learned on my heartfulness journey and offer some final words of insight. Slaying dragons may seem violent but is necessary to conquer our deepest fears. In particular because I was taught through religion the "polly-annie" way of dealing with life's darkest moments.

In my Latino culture I was also taught to be silent and not make any waves and in society as a woman of color I was told to keep my head down and shut-up and color. I had to learn on my own and through the guidance of my hearts intuition that fierce opposition must be meet with the same level of positive opposition. This is not a simple undertaking. The late Dr. Martin Luther King said it best "Darkness cannot drive out darkness; only light can do that. Hate cannot drive out hate; only love can do that." When I talk about slaying dragons, I talk about slaying them with the sword of love and compassion and heartfulness which make better weapons than any other kind.

As an educated Latina professional, I've learned the power of taking control of my health and my life. When I faced a serious illness that brought me to my deathbed, I knew that relying solely on confidence and fairy dust was not enough. I had to take action and do the deep work of slaying the mammoth dragons that threatened to consume me. This battle against illness and fear is not unique to me, but a universal struggle faced by many. Even some of history's greatest minds, like Albert Einstein, recognized the importance of this fight. He quoted a biblical passage to convey the idea that our true enemies are not physical, but spiritual: "For we wrestle not against flesh and blood, but against principalities, against powers, against the rulers of the darkness of this world, against spiritual wickedness in high places" (Ephesians 6:12, KJV).

This passage reminds us that we must fight against the negative forces that threaten to overwhelm us, whether they come from within or without. In this day and age these forces come from the daily toxic news, social media, and endless marketing ads about how sick we are and how we must rely on pharmaceuticals to heal instead of tuning in to our own unique body's ability to heal. The forces are also our narrow understanding of how the human body works and how energy is influential in all areas of our lives both in the physical realms and the spiritual realms. In the disciplines of physics, of which I don't claim to be well versed in, I know the double slit experiment, originally conducted by scientists in the field of quantum physics such as Thomas Young and later replicated by many others, has provided me with a deeper understanding of how our perceptions as observers can have a profound impact on shaping our realities.

I also understand the power of the collective due to Lynne McTaggart's book, "The Power of Eight"[2] in which she explores the idea that the act of sending positive intentions to others can have a profound impact on both the sender and the receiver. Through scientific research and real-life case studies, McTaggart demonstrates how the power of group intention can lead to healing, abundance, and greater connection. She argues that the key to harnessing this power is through the creation of intention groups, where individuals come together to focus their collective intention on a shared goal. The book provides practical guidance on how to form and run these groups, as well as insights into the spiritual and scientific implications of this phenomenon. Overall, "The Power of Eight" offers a compelling argument for the transformative power of intention and the potential for collective consciousness to bring about positive change in the world.

Across many religions and belief systems, there is a shared recognition that we must engage in this battle for the sake of our own wellbeing. We must actively seek to heal ourselves and our souls, not passively waiting for someone

---

[2] https://lynnemctaggart.com/books/the-power-of-eight/

else to do it for us. We must be resolute in the fight, knowing that slaying the dragons and overcoming our fears is necessary for our own growth and happiness.

With this mindset and the courage to take action, we can overcome any obstacle that comes our way and emerge stronger and more resilient than ever before. We must never forget that we have the power to overcome even the greatest challenges, as long as we are willing to do the deep work of healing ourselves and our souls.

Similar passages in other world religions include:

Hinduism: "The real enemies are lust, anger, greed, attachment, and ego, which reside within us" (Bhagavad Gita 3.37).

Buddhism: "Our real enemies are our own defilements, not external foes. Anger, attachment, and ignorance are the true adversaries" (Dhammapada 3.1).

Islam: "Verily Satan is an enemy to you: so, treat him as an enemy. He only invites his adherents, that they may become Companions of the Blazing Fire" (Quran 35:6).

Judaism: "For we do not wrestle against flesh and blood, but against principalities, against powers, against the rulers of the darkness of this age, against spiritual hosts of wickedness in the heavenly places" (Ephesians 6:12, KJV) - This passage is shared by both Judaism and Christianity.

Sikhism: "The real enemy is your own ego and the five vices within you" (Sri Guru Granth Sahib).

Throughout my life, I have faced many challenges that have tested my resolve and pushed me to the brink of despair. Whether it was my Catholic upbringing or my evangelical Christian beliefs, fear was a constant companion in my life. It was not until I embraced heartfulness that I was able to break free from the shackles of fear and live a more fulfilling life.

Heartfulness is more than just a way of thinking; <u>it is a way of being.</u> It involves aligning our thoughts and actions with the wisdom of our hearts and tapping into the power of the universe to bring about positive change. It means slaying the dragons of fear and doubt with a heartfulness daily practice and embracing the unknown with courage and hope.

One of the key lessons I have learned on my heartfulness journey is the importance of listening to the wisdom within our hearts. Our hearts have their own rhythms and can guide us through life if we are willing to listen. It is through heartful listening that we can tap into the divine and bring about positive change in our lives.

Another lesson I have learned is the importance of simplicity and mentorship. Simplicity involves living a life that is free from unnecessary distractions and focusing on what truly matters. Mentorship involves seeking out those who have walked the path before us and learning from their wisdom and experience.

Finally, I want to leave you with a message of hope. No matter what challenges you may be facing in your life, know that you have the power to overcome them. You have a heartful heart that is filled with wisdom, courage, and hope. Use it to slay the dragons of fear and doubt, and embrace a life of love, peace, and freedom.

I want to thank you for joining me on this heartful journey. I hope that my words have inspired you to embrace heartfulness and live a more fulfilling life. Remember, you have the power to slay dragons, both high and low and whether or not these dragons reside simply in your head or the real dragons that wait for us out in the real world never doubt you were built for this moment.

May your heart be filled with love, peace, and hope always and may your understanding of the heart-mind connection help you feel your heart and grow rich.

EPILOGUE

It's hard to believe that I've poured out so many words onto this page (or keyboard, really) in such a short amount of time, but I know deep down that it will all be worth it if just one person is touched by my words. Gone are the days when I obsessed over perfect grammar and sentence structure, paralyzed by the fear of being judged for not having proper English.

I still remember the college professor who ridiculed me for writing "inglish" instead of English, because for me it sounded the same in Spanish. But I've since forgiven those who tried to suppress my eagerness to be part of this wonderful country (USA) and learn it's language, who tried to dim my light, and to crush my heart and soul for being too bilingual, too sensitive, too liberal, or too kind.

What's truly important is that I've written this book from the heart, and that I've been honest and truthful about my pain and joy. These are the things that connect us as human beings. We are a complex and fragile species, full of intricate nuances and mystical qualities worth exploring. I have love and compassion for all of us as we journey on this tiny blue planet, sustained by the fabric of dark matter, perhaps even love itself. It's not important to know how or why, but to simply recognize that we are love and that it has the power to heal, repair, and evolve us. Wealth and happiness are possible through the heart-mind connection, and I hope that readers never doubt this.

May you be blessed every day of your life.

With love and sincerity,

Adriana

RESOURCES

As I reflect on my journey to recovery, I am overwhelmed with gratitude for the kind and compassionate spiritual healers who have helped me along the way. Their unwavering support and guidance have been invaluable to me, and I am deeply thankful for the positive impact they have had on my life.

Their expertise, empathy, and dedication to healing have been instrumental in my journey towards inner peace and self-discovery. I encourage anyone in need of spiritual guidance to seek out their services and experience the transformative power of their healing practices firsthand.

My very first encounter with the truly mystical was **Lee Papa**. She was the first spiritual coach and initiated me on this path. https://leepapa.com

I continued to learn more about my ability to tap into my spiritual self with my Reiki teacher **Jodie Friedman.** www.intentionalhealings.com

My journey also took me to meet **Ani Williams** a world-renowned sound healer who has more than two-dozen albums of original music based on ancient spiritual traditions. She has done seminal work in the study of sound, the relationship between musical tones, the human voice and healing. (Willimas, 2023) https://aniwilliams.com/

I reached out to a practitioner from the Body Code practitioner **Maria Ruiz**, who help me identify what energy was stuck in my body. https://discoverhealing.com/staff-practitioners/mary

As I continued to discover how I was connected to the other side I reached out to **Marla Frees**, www.marlafrees.com: She helped me connect with my father and grandfather. (Frees, 2023)

I continued to practice the six phases by **Vishen Lakhiani** https://www.mindvalley.com/learn-meditation

I also continue to learn from Gary Weber and his form of meditation. https://happiness-beyond-thought.com/disclaimer

Some of the most power ways of shifting your mindset to understand the world different is via **Gregg Braden'** work in particular his medication you can find here: https://greggbraden.com/video

As I continued my journey with discovering alternative ways to heal my physical body I reached out to **Corina Bautista**. She is a meditation and sound healing instructor and a wellness advocate. My sound session with her was so revealing that I was able to realign my energy centers and her complete assessment of what was going on with me energetically. https://vivayalive.com/guides/393/corina-bautista

In my initial health crisis, I reached out to my dear friend **Edie O'Reilly**, author of the book When the Body Speaks: A practical 3 Step Guide to Happiness. Her book can be found on Amazon here: https://amzn.to/3YFvrAQ

I also want to mention *Kim Babcock* author of the book Inside Out: A Journey to Inner Peace. I had a one-hour session with her where she helped me identify some unhealthy thought patters I was repeating and also help me understand that the way I was thinking was getting in the way of my full recovery. I'm eternally grateful for her insight. Her work is brilliant, and my heart is full of appreciation. You can check out her book here: https://amzn.to/3T7dU3s

Just minutes before publication of this book I felt intuitively I needed to add my friend *Cristen Lyn Jacobsen* who passed away January of last year 2022. I had the privilege of knowing her and on many occasions, she would show up on my walks as a "dragonfly" a reminder of how we first met. She was my spiritual sister and her philanthropic work lives on. Here is the nonprofit she worked so hard to create: https://hope4hearts.org/donate/

Throughout my arduous journey towards healing, I was blessed to receive the unwavering support and dedication of numerous medical doctors at the Mike O'Callaghan Military Medical Center. Despite the challenges inherent in diagnosing my symptoms, they spared no effort in their pursuit of an accurate diagnosis.

As I reflect on this journey, I cannot help but recognize the profound significance of the connections I formed with each person mentioned above. Each one of them shared a piece of themselves with me, offering kindness and compassion in abundance. It is my belief that this is why we are here on earth - to express our love and compassion for one another.

Writing about this experience fills my heart with joy, and I am honored to share my gratitude for these remarkable individuals who played such a vital role in my recovery.

Bibliography

Atwater, D. P. (2023, March 1). *Dr. PMH Atwater*. Retrieved from
    Atwater: http://pmhatwater.com/

Braden, G. (2023, March 1). *Gregg Braden*. Retrieved from Gregg Braden:
    https://greggbraden.com/press/the-god-code-message-
    encoded-as-the-dna-of-life-science-to-sage-2014/

Cox, J. (2023, January 1). *JC Cox*. Retrieved from International Medical
    Qigong College:
    https://www.medicalqigong.org/index.php/directory/us-
    directory/10-jc-cox

Frees, M. (2023, January 11). *Marla Frees*. Retrieved from Marla Frees :
    https://amzn.to/3YXnEyx

HearMath. (2023, March 7). *HeartMath* . Retrieved from HeartMath :
    https://www.heartmath.org/research/

Mate, D. G. (2023, March 1). *Dr. Gabor Mate*. Retrieved from Dr Gabor
    Mate: https://amzn.to/3J1ABBo

Myss, C. (2023, March 1). *Book Anatomy of the Spirit*. Retrieved from
    Books : https://amzn.to/3ylV1Am

Rudd, R. (2023, January 1). *Gene Keys*. Retrieved from Gene Keys:
    https://genekeys.com/

Willimas, A. (2023, January 1). *Ani Willimas* . Retrieved from Ani Williams:
    https://aniwilliams.com/

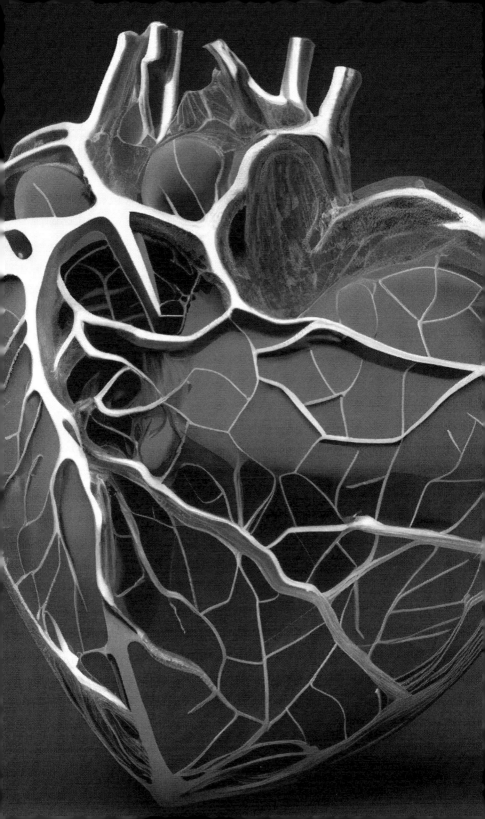

You may give us a review at:

https://www.amazon.com/review/create-review/?ie=UTF8&channel=glance-detail&asin=B0BY64Z3V4

My Gracie 2018

Made in the USA
Columbia, SC
06 February 2024

97098c33-74b3-40c6-b619-66d2d424a85bR01